MW00449675

DEATH, DYING, AND BEREAVEMENT AROUND THE WORLD

DEATH, DYING, AND BEREAVEMENT AROUND THE WORLD

Theories, Varied Views and Customs

By

FRANK E. EYETSEMITAN, Ph.D.

Professor of Psychology
Roger Williams University

CHARLES C THOMAS · PUBLISHER · LTD.
Springfield · Illinois · U.S.A.

Published and Distributed Throughout the World by

CHARLES C THOMAS • PUBLISHER, LTD.
2600 South First Street
Springfield, Illinois 62704

This book is protected by copyright. No part of
it may be reproduced in any manner without written
permission from the publisher. All rights reserved.

© 2021 by CHARLES C THOMAS • PUBLISHER, LTD.

ISBN 978-0-398-09348-8 (paper)
ISBN 978-0-398-09349-5 (ebook)

Library of Congress Catalog Card Number: 2020038961 (print)
2020038962 (ebook)

With THOMAS BOOKS c*areful attention is given to all details of manufacturing
and design. It is the Publisher's desire to present books that are satisfactory as to their
physical qualities and artistic possibilities and appropriate for their particular use.*
THOMAS BOOKS *will be true to those laws of quality that assure a good name
and good will.*

Printed in the United States of America
MM-C-1

Library of Congress Cataloging-in-Publication Data

Names: Eyetsemitan, Frank E., 1955– author.
Title: Death, dying, bereavement around the world : theories, varied
   views and customs / by Frank E. Eyetsemitan, Ph.D., Professor of
   Psychology, Roger Williams University.
Description: Springfield, Illinois : Charles C Thomas, Publisher, Ltd.,
   [2021] | Includes bibliographical references and index.
Identifiers: LCCN 2020038961 (print) | LCCN 2020038962 (ebook) |
   ISBN 9780398093488 (paperback) | ISBN 9780398093495 (ebook)
Subjects: LCSH: Death. | Bereavement.
Classification: LCC HQ1073 .E94 2021 (print) | LCC HQ1073 (ebook)
   | DDC 306.9–dc23
LC record available at https://lccn.loc.gov/2020038961
LC ebook record available at https://lccn.loc.gov/2020038962

PREFACE

This book reviews death, dying and bereavement from around the world—from both developed (technologically advanced) and developing (not-so-technologically advanced) societies; also, from societies that are more culturally Individualistic versus societies that are more Collectivistic. Developed societies (mostly Western societies) have been dominant in defining death, dying and bereavement processes. How pan-cultural are these? In this book, varied customs and practices in death, dying and bereavement from around the world are reviewed and contributions made to existing theories/models.

Due to Westernization influences people in non-Western societies tend to display "accommodation" behavior; they embrace aspects of Western culture yet maintain their traditional cultural practices. For example, in accommodation behavior, there is a dual belief in Western medicine and in traditional beliefs about death causation. A dual belief in Western autopsy report and in "evil eye" as a cause for death may produce an interesting grief recovery process.

A compelling reason for writing this book is to evaluate existing theories/concepts/models with the practices of death, dying and bereavement from different societies around the world. Also, being a single author's work maintaining a consistent theme throughout the book becomes easier. In the book an overview of countries in different continents is provided. This helps to refresh the reader's mind of the country's geographical location and also brings attention to the prevailing causes of death, and life expectancy of nations in different parts of the world. The difference in different belief systems and how they influence death, dying and bereavement practices in different parts of the world are also highlighted, including Hinduism, Christianity, Islam, Ancestor Worship, Afro-Brazilian religions, the belief systems of Native Indians, and of the Maoris of New Zealand and others. These belief systems are able to make contributions to existing models of death, dying and bereavement which is brought forth in this book.

This book is suitable as either a stand-alone or a supplementary text for a course on death, dying and bereavement. At the end of each chapter review questions to aid the reader's comprehension and self-refection are provided. Furthermore, with the section on Additional Readings, the reader is able to find additional information to further an interest developed from reading the chapter material. A glossary of terms is also included to aid with not just with explaining certain terms, but also adding to the reader's vocabulary on issues pertaining to death, dying and bereavement in different parts of the world. Given its overview of existing theories/models as well as a focus on issues of cross-cultural relevance on death, dying and bereavement, the book will also be of much interest for self-help, to bereavement counselors, and to healthcare practitioners.

In Chapter 1, an overview of the world as having developed and developing nations is provided, based on the UN criteria of per capita gross domestic products (GDP), share of manufacturing in total GDP, adult literacy rate, augmented quality of life index, economic diversification index, and population size. This classification has implications for prevalent factors responsible for death and dying in different countries.

Also, cultural differences between developed (mostly Western) and developing (mostly non-Western) countries have implications on matters concerning death, dying and bereavement. For example, Western cultures are more individualistic, whereas non-Western cultures are more collectivistic. However, Western value systems are also influential in non-Western societies, e.g., Western medicine and Western education. Therefore, among non-Westerners "accommodation behavior" is common—that is, maintaining both Western and non-Western beliefs (e.g., accepting Western medical autopsy report on death causation and traditional beliefs about "evil eye" as responsible for death) at the same time.

In Chapter 2, different theories and models on bereavement are discussed. Some are descriptive (what to expect as normal or abnormal behaviors), whereas others are prescriptive (what actions to take unto recovery). They include grief work, complicated grief or prolonged grief disorder, and coping with a loss, among others. Stress accompanying a loss is also discussed, because it could result in mental health issues, including depression. The perception of stress as either a threat or a challenge with implications for coping and growth are presented.

Chapter 3 presents an overview of countries in Africa, their life expectancy and prevailing causes of death. Most Africans are believers in Christianity, Islam and/or Ancestor Worship (Traditional African religion). They are also dual believers, e.g., Christianity or Islam and Ancestor Worship. The implications of the complexity of belief systems on death, dying and bereavement practices as well as Westernization influences are discussed.

Chapter 4 presents an overview of countries of the Middle East region, including life expectancy and prevailing causes of death. Islam, being the dominant religion in the region, and its teachings has an impact on how issues surrounding death, dying and bereavement are addressed, as well as how Westernization influences are embraced.

Chapter 5 reviews the religions, the predominant causes of death and the life expectancy of countries of North America (including the Central American region). Christianity is the dominant religion in the US, Canada and Mexico—countries that make up 85% of the population of the region. There are also minority ethnic group members and practitioners of indigenous religions that reflect on death, dying and bereavement practices differently. The minority ethnic group members are mostly collectivistic in culture, but they exhibit accommodation behavior, also.

Chapter 6 presents an overview of the nations of South America, their predominant death causing factors and life expectancy. Christianity is the dominant religion, but practices of other religions by minority ethnic group members who also exhibit accommodation behavior in death and dying practices, are common. Among minority ethnic group members based on the belief in the ability of the deceased to do good or harm to the living, attention is given the deceased in ensuring he or she is provided a "proper" burial, in accordance with laid down tradition. Focus on the deceased's needs during and after burial is important to the grief recovery process.

The focus in Chapter 7 is on the nations of Asia, the largest continent, including their life expectancy and prevailing causes of death. Asia is also the most populous continent in the world and has several countries with life expectancy above 80 years, including Japan with the highest at 85.30 years. Asia has numerous religions, but Islam, Hinduism, Buddhism Sikhism and Christianity are the dominant ones. The vast majority of practitioners of Hinduism and Buddhism are in Asia. Discussions are presented on how these religions are influential in death, dying and bereavement practices.

Chapter 8 presents the nations of Europe, including their life expectancy and prevailing causes of death. There is a decline in "religiosity" in Europe, including in Italy the seat of the Roman Catholic church with a following of 2.1 billion people worldwide. The chapter discusses how religious decline could rekindle old practices in death, dying and bereavement.

Chapter 9 focuses on the region of Oceania, including the predominant causes of death and life expectancy of the nations in the area. Australia is the largest country with a predominant Caucasian and Christian population. Indigenous Australians (or Aboriginals) make up about 3.3% of Australia's population and have different belief systems that see everything as interconnected—birth, death, the lands and elements of nature. They believe in an afterlife, where the deceased person joins the ancestors in spirit form and provides guidance to the living. New Zealand's population, mostly of European descent (70%) and Christian, is also racially diverse. It has indigenous people (the largest being the Maoris) who have similar beliefs to the indigenous people of Australia. The indigenous people exhibit accommodation behavior by professing Christianity but also holding on to traditional practices.

Chapter 10 considers factors likely to make possible contributions to existing models/theories from reviewing death, dying and bereavement practices around the world. Such factors include the influence of religion; the impact of individualism versus collectivism, traditional/cultural practices; and accommodation behavior, among others.

Chapter 11 considers the types of help available to a dying person, including physician-assisted suicide, euthanasia, death tourism, living will, palliative care, traditional medicine and death doulas. It also discusses factors likely to influence how dying persons choose to spend their remainder time on earth. Such factors include if a dying person has accepted that death is imminent, if the dying person's health status enables travel or not, how the dying person wishes to be remembered, mending relationships, taking care of unfinished businesses and keeping their house in order.

Chapter 12 identifies common themes and differences from reviewing death, dying and bereavement around the world. They include factors that would influence the decision on death such as available medical resources, beliefs systems, cultural orientation and personal preferences. While the predominant factors of death causation might vary across nations of the world, the important impact of cross-border infectious diseases like COVID-19 is also highlighted. Also, an interesting trend to note in the future is more people are opting for cremation over earth burial and the advocacy of environmentally friendly people for green burial and cremation. However, religion still plays an important role in choosing between conventional or unconventional funeral and burial practices in different parts of the world.

F. E.

CONTENTS

DEATH, DYING, AND BEREAVEMENT AROUND THE WORLD

Chapter 1

THEMES AND ISSUES IN DEATH, DYING AND BEREAVEMENT AROUND THE WORLD

Chapter Outline

Learning Objectives
Developed and developing worlds: organizing framework
Collectivism versus Individualism
Collectivism versus individualism: cognitive styles
Influence of individualism (Westernization) on death, dying and
    bereavement
Cultural values
The "triarchical" dimensions of non-Western societies
The individual and the triarchical environmental dimensions
Group self-esteem and triarchical environmental dimensions
Definition of death across cultures
The social meaning of death
Euthanasia/Good death
Death location
The concept of dying
Living will
Beliefs about death causation
Summary
Key terms
Review questions
Additional readings

Learning Objectives

LO1: Examine the definition of death globally

LO2: Understand cultural factors that differentiate Western developed societies from non- Western developing societies

LO3: Explain Accommodation behavior

LO4: Describe the environmental dimensions of non-Western developing societies

LO5: Explain collectivism and individualism in death and dying practices

DEVELOPED AND DEVELOPING WORLDS: ORGANIZING FRAMEWORK

This chapter highlights the differences between the developed and the developing worlds— as context for analyzing the global relevance of theories, models and concepts of death, dying and bereavement. According to the UN (2019: https://www.un.org/development /desa/dpad/wp-content/uploads/sites/45/WESP2019_BOOK-ANNEX -en.pdf), the developing world is comprised of countries in the regions of Asia (excluding Japan), North America (excluding Canada and the United States), South America, Africa, and Oceania (excluding Australia and New Zealand). In terms of "development" however, countries in the developing world are not at the same level just as nations of the developed world, also. Thus, there is a continuum of development, to be discussed later.

The United Nations (2019) uses the following as criteria for development:

- Per capita gross domestic products (GDP)
- Share of manufacturing in total GDP
- Adult literacy rate,
- Augmented quality of life index,
- Economic diversification index, and
- Population size.

Differences in the prevalent causes of death across the world are tied to socio-economic development classifications. The World Bank has its own classification, which will be addressed in later chapters, also. Socio-economic factors aside, other factors help to differentiate non-Western developing societies from Western developed societies. They include cognitive styles and behaviors that have implications for death, dying, and bereavement practices.

Collectivism versus Individualism

Geert Hostede's (1980) concept of collectivism versus individualism provides an organizing framework in differentiating developing (mostly non-Western) societies from developed (mostly Western) societies. These differences are reflected in biomedical advancements, in defining death, in bereavement outcomes, and in other death and dying related issues. The chapter also, discusses the global impact of Westernization influences among non-Westerners resulting in "accommodation behavior." Accommodation behavior is having both Western and non-Western thoughts and actions, which can influence death, dying and bereavement practices. Accommodation behavior may not be captured in current theories and models on death, dying and bereavement which were developed among Western populations.

Death is universal and happens everywhere but between the developed and developing societies it happens more in the latter where, due to poor health care and a lack of advanced biomedical technology, life expectancy is shorter resulting in a higher frequency of death across the lifespan. However, Western developed societies have been in the fore-front in developing theories and concepts on death, dying and bereavement.

In 20th century North America a "death culture" is based on long life expectancy, on perceived control over the forces of nature and on individualism (e.g., Morgan, 1995). This assertion is likely true of other Western developed societies. However, what shapes "death culture" in non-Western developing societies may be different. Given that attitudes, beliefs and behaviors influence death practices, the death culture in non-Western developing societies may be influenced by a shorter life expectancy, a lack of perceived control over death and collectivism. However, with Westernization influences around the world the death culture in non-Western societies may be impacted, as well.

Collectivism vs Individualism: Cognitive Styles

Geert Hofstede's (1980) work on collectivism and individualism helps in differentiating the cognitive styles of non-Westerners from Westerners. Non-Westerners tend to be more collectivistic emphasizing interdependence, relatedness, and social obligation in values. Westerners, however, are more individualistic with a tendency toward independence, self-containment, and autonomy (Billing et al., 2014; Caffaro, Ferraris, & Schmidt, 2014; Finkelstein, 2012). Furthermore, they value equality, freedom, and an exciting lifestyle whereas collectivists appreciate social order, honoring of parents and elders, and self-discipline (Schwartz & Bilsky, 1990). Researcher Harry Triandis (1995) anchors the collectivism-individualism construct on the following four universal dimensions:

Definition of self: Collectivists view self in relation to others, with interdependency in resource sharing whereas Individualists view self as autonomous from groups, with no obligation to share resources and make decisions individually.

Structure of goals: in collectivist cultures individual goals are subsumed within in-group goals. The in-group is made up of a person or persons you feel similar to such as sharing a common fate or some other attributes e.g., caste, kin, race, tribe, religion, village, nation. Membership of an ingroup is ascribed but not earned unlike the individualist's in-group which is generally achieved e.g., similar beliefs, attitudes, values, actions, programs, occupation. In individualist cultures the individual's goals and ambitions supersede those of the in-group, most times.

Emphasis on norms versus personal beliefs: In collectivist cultures emphasis is on norms, duties, and obligations in determining social behavior whereas in individualist cultures what determines social behavior are attitudes, personal needs, perceived rights, and contracts.

Emphasis on relatedness versus rationality: Collectivist cultures emphasize relatedness whereas individualist cultures emphasize rationality. In relatedness priority is given to relationships even if not to the individual's advantage whereas with rationality emphasis is placed on the transactional cost/ benefit of relationships.

Influence of Individualism (Westernization) on Death, Dying & Bereavement

Most theories and models on death, dying and bereavement are developed in the Western world. Therefore, the individualistic values/cognitive styles play major roles in the following:

a) Advance directive/living will—which enables individuals to have control over end-of-life decisions affecting them.
b) Industrialization of death, dying and bereavement—which allows for choice-making with services and products provided by casket manufacturers, morticians, funeral directors, funeral homes, grief counselors, hospice care providers and healthcare workers.
c) Physician-assisted suicide /euthanasia—which allows for individual choice making in not continuing with living when faced with a terminal illness and suffering.

Cultural Values

Closely aligned with Geert Hofstede's (1980) work on individualism and collectivism is Shalom Schwartz's (2007) work on cultural values. Values are the implicit beliefs that act as guiding principles toward achieving goals, at both personal and group levels. Schwartz (2007) researched Values in 80 countries in every continent of the world. To a group or a person, some values are more important than others. For example, conformity is valued more by Nigerians and Indonesians than Germans and Swedes (e.g., Schwartz, 1994, 2017). Schwartz (2007) identified seven cultural value orientations and summarized them in three polar opposite dimensions:

Autonomy versus Embeddedness. In cultures that value Autonomy people are boundless in expressing their thoughts, and are encouraged to express their ideas, feelings and preferences. There are two types of Autonomy: cognitive autonomy and emotional/affective autonomy. In cognitive autonomy the individual is encouraged to think independently of others and to pursue own ideas; whereas in emotional/affective autonomy regarding death and dying, for example, people can express how they wish to be buried, how they wish to be remembered, or they can make decisions on extending life support or not, irrespective of others' feelings. In autonomy culture people strive to be unique, and it is in the context of this uniqueness that the Western definition of personality is derived. In defining personality, the American Psychological Association (APA, n.d.) puts it this way: "[I]ndividual differences in characteristic patterns of thinking, feeling and behaving" (American Psychological Association: https://www.apa.org/topics/personality/ n.d.). However, studies show that in cultures (Western societies) where independence is valued above inter-independence people tend to enhance the self at the expense of others, whereas in inter-dependent cultures (non-Western societies) this tendency is less common, as the desire to conform to the traditional ways of doing things holds sway (e.g., Kitayama et al., 2006). Therefore, in defining personality in non-Western societies *individual differences* may not be the *raison d'être* in such cultures. In cultures high on independence people may decide on what type of funeral they wish to have or who they wish to attend or not attend their funeral. In societies that value interdependence, however, it is difficult to restrict the number of funeral attendees or who not to allow, as such action may go against social norms or cultural expectations.

Egalitarianism vs. Hierarchy: In Egalitarian societies (mostly Western) people are socialized to treat and respect each other as equals, whereas in hierarchical societies (mostly non-Western), people are socialized to respect age, gender and status. In the order of things children are given the least respect, and males command more respect than females. Although banned by the government *Sati* is the Indian tradition whereby the widow throws herself into the funeral pyre of her deceased husband, as a demonstration of her devotion to her deceased spouse. However, the husband does not reciprocate this action for his deceased wife, reflecting a hierarchical status of males over females.

Mastery vs. Harmony: In mastery cultures (e.g., Western societies), people try to make changes to the natural world to suit their purpose. For example, they prefer to have choices on how and when to die (e.g., physician-assisted suicide or euthanasia). In Harmony cultures (e.g., non-Western societies), however, people understand that the best way to live is to blend their lives with others and nature, and that a disruption of such could lead to illness or death. Therefore, little is done to change or interrupt the natural environment.

Shalom Schwartz (2007) notes that cultural values change little, even in the midst of political and social changes. However, some people are likely to embrace change, while others hold on the old ways.

Yet, others embrace new values and hold on to old traditional values, at the same time; a phenomenon known as "accommodation" behavior e.g., a belief in both Western medical autopsy report and a belief in disruption of natural harmony, as responsible for death.

THE "TRIARCHICAL" DIMENSIONS
OF NON-WESTERN SOCIETIES

The environment of non-Western societies is not monolithic; it is made up of a triarchical dimension: 1) Global—these are universal biological imperatives that all humans share in e.g., biological changes at the cellular level, emotions; 2) Developed/Western: Westernization influences, e.g., Western medicine; and 3) Developing/non-Western, e.g., indigenous cultural beliefs about natural harmony (Eyetsemitan & Gire, 2003).

The Global Dimension is worldwide, such as the biological experience of death and dying that is shared by everyone. The emotion of sadness accompanying a loss which is biologically wired is also a worldwide experience (cf. Ekman & Friesen, 1986). Also, is the universal biological imperative (known as senescence) that propels a gradual decline in natural abilities which is unidirectional and leads to cell damage, loss, harm or organ failure (Yates & Benton, 1995). This is a reason why across all societies, death is not expected in childhood but later in life.

Worldwide, Westernization Influences are more dominant than non-Western cultural artifacts and belief systems (e.g., Eyetsemitan & Gire, 2003). Dominant Western cultural elements include industrialization, education, medicine and modern technology. In death and dying Western medical approaches include embalming, autopsy, and organ donation. Westernization influences can be both positive and negative, however. Whereas Western medicine help to elongate life (e.g., vaccines), Western technology and industrialization can speed up death through automobile accidents and industrial pollution, which are common in non-Western societies. According to the WHO (2020), whereas developing countries account for 60% of the world's registered vehicles, they nonetheless contribute to the largest share (93%) of deaths resulting from worldwide automobile accidents.

With Westernization influences, however, non-Western Indigenous cultural practices do persist. They include native medicine, spiritualism, native religion, simple technology and collectivism (see Eyetsemitan & Gire, 2003 for details). Also, death is defined culturally, including mourning rituals, estate disposal, spiritual autopsy, death language, and symbolic immortality.

THE INDIVIDUAL AND THE TRIARCHICAL ENVIRONMENTAL DIMENSIONS

An individual can interface with one or more of the triarchical dimensions either voluntarily or involuntarily (see Eyetsemitan & Gire, 2003 for details). When an individual's behavior exhibits influences from more than one dimension, "accommodation" behavior is said to result (e.g., Western and Indigenous). For example, in Botswana a study of health-seeking behavior and attitudes among 212 tuberculosis (TB) patients found that patients used modern medicine for symptom relief (Western), but also sought traditional treatment because they believed that the breaking of taboos (Tswana) was the cause of TB (Steen & Mazonde, 1999). Close to 80% of African patients are dual users of Western medicine and traditional healing practices (e.g., Graham et al., 2013).

GROUP SELF-ESTEEM AND TRIARCHICAL ENVIRONMENTAL DIMENSIONS

A sense of self-worth is derived from group membership (e.g., ethnic, race or nationality). Therefore, a group self-esteem may be a determinant factor in rejecting the influence of a foreign culture. Based on a high group self-esteem, an individual may retain identification with own culture and reject identification with a foreign culture, whereas the opposite would result from a low group self-esteem, leading to a rejection of own culture and embracing a foreign culture, instead (e.g., Berry, 2006).

DEFINITION OF DEATH ACROSS CULTURES

Based on technological advancement, the definition or pronouncement of death may differ across societies. Death is best defined as brain death, and characterized by profound coma, apnea and absence of all brain-stem reflexes (Setzer, 1985; Taylor, 1997). And with this definition organ donation and transplantation procedure can commence (e.g., Lazar et al., 2001). This definition is a marked departure from the traditional cardiopulmonary criteria still in use in many developing societies, where the number of neurologists per capita of population is one in three million people (e.g., Baumgartner & Gerstenbrand, 2002).

The Social Meaning of Death

With death comes an end to biological functioning, but so also are any type of social roles and activities that the deceased had participated in, including being a parent, brother, uncle, friend, co-worker, etc. Organic definition of death does not supplant a cultural or social understanding of life's cessation (Gervais, 1989; Jones, 1998; Sass, 1992). In non-Western cultures (and Western cultures) social bonds are maintained with deceased loved ones, who in the afterlife assume new roles and activities that are more powerful than their earthly ones. In spirit form the deceased in the afterlife is perceived to possess supernatural powers to do good or evil to earthly beings. In some Western grief models (e.g., Worden 2008), however, it is suggested that the survivor should move on from the loss, while memorializing the deceased.

Euthanasia/Good Death

Originally coined from the Greek word, euthanasia means "good death" (e.g., Annadurai, Danasekaran, & Mani, 2014). In the face of growing biomedical technology that sustains life but not necessarily its quality, the concept of "good death" has taken on an important meaning in Western societies. The question to be asked is, who or what defines life: technology or humans? In developing societies, with poor technological advancement, technology plays a minimal or to no role in defining "good death."

In Western societies death has a legal status for organ donation or life insurance payments to beneficiaries to be effected (e.g., Taylor, 1997). In non-Western societies the pronouncement of death is influenced by cultural factors, especially in rural areas. This includes a process of informing community elders (who may not be immediate kin) thereby delaying organ donation, where time is of the essence. This is reminiscent of collectivism.

DEATH LOCATION

Death in Western technologically advanced societies mostly occurs outside of the home (e.g., in hospital, nursing homes or assisted living facilities). However, death in many developing countries occurs mostly in locations outside of medical facilities because of acute illnesses or accidents that result in mortality. Furthermore, a contributing factor is the lack of adequate medical facilities.

Ironically, whereas in technologically advanced societies people prefer to die at home, in less technologically advanced societies citizens prefer to die in Western medical facilities, signifying that the best help to save their lives was sought after. Medical tourism to Western countries is a growing behavior among affluent non-Westerners in developing societies. For example, in 2017 the Nigerian president Mohammed Buhari spent almost two months (19 January to 10 March) receiving medical treatment in a UK hospital (e.g., BBC, 2017: https://www.bbc.com/news/world-africa-39842686).

THE CONCEPT OF DYING

Not all societies agree on the concept of dying. In Western societies the pronouncement of "dying" falls under the purview of a medical doctor—usually after a medical examination and with further medical opinions. In the South Pacific, however, Counts and Counts (1985) report on cultural beliefs about dying. Dying is believed to occur with "life force" gradually leaving the body when a person is asleep or is suffering from a very serious illness. In Micronesia, the Trukese also hold similar beliefs that life ends when a person is forty, after which dying begins. Conceivably in the absence of advanced medical technology, physical strength and agility are the yardsticks for determining the dying process. Anticipatory grief could commence during the dying process of a loved one. But it is not clear if anticipatory grief follows a culturally determined process (instead of a medically determined decision) of dying.

Living Will

A dying person may be limited in making decisions by themselves, cognitively. Therefore, a living will, which is a written instrument made beforehand, is executed by a dying person (called the principal) permitting another person (called the agent or attorney) to act on their behalf if unable to make such a decision in the future (e.g., Braun, Pietsch & Blanchette, 1999). The principal further determines if the agent's power should be durable (continues in the case of mental incapacitation), non-durable (ceases after mental incapacitation stops) or 'springing" (to take effect at some future date).

In the absence of an advanced directive, the legal default surrogate decision maker is the spouse; and if no spouse, a family member falls next in line, and if no family member exists, the decision falls on a friend (e.g., Braun, Pietsch & Blanchette, 1999).

In non-Western collectivist societies, however, age, gender, and level of education would have considerable weight on behalf of a dying loved one in making end-of-life decision. The young are likely to defer to the old, females to males, and the uneducated to the educated. Generally, family members have a perceived right in matters affecting their kin—similar to group membership being more important than the individual in collectivistic cultures (e.g., Eyetsemitan & Gire, 2003).

BELIEFS ABOUT DEATH CAUSATION

Whereas cause of death could be objectively identified (e.g., heart attack), beliefs about death causation may differ. Beliefs are important because they affect help seeking behavior. Most times, in non-Western societies beliefs about death causation are spiritually based, and are due to sorcery, evil eye or witchcraft (e.g., Fottrell et al., 2012). Fottrell et al. (2012) note that medical registration for the causes of death is rare and witchcraft is attributed as cause to premature deaths. In Ghana, the ratio of traditional healing practitioners to the total population is 1:200 and medical doctors to the total population is 1:20,000, thus making attributions to supernatural causes for death more common. In Swaziland attributions to witchcraft are made for death causation, also. The ratio of traditional healers to the total population is 1:100; and that of medical doctors to the total population is 1:10,000 (Conserve Africa, 2002).

With the inadequate number of pathologists to verify death, cultural beliefs about death causation or "verbal autopsy" becomes a common phenomenon (Fottrell et al., 2012). In verbal autopsy, death causation is based on signs and symptoms of the deceased prior to death, coupled with lay opinions. Usually, a "spiritual" post-mortem examination by a native doctor or a spiritualist on the cause of death, is preferred because the native doctor or spiritualist could provide recommendations to avoid future deaths, e.g., maintaining harmony with nature or the spirit world.

SUMMARY

1. Countries of the world are not at the same level of socioeconomic development. Based on the UN, some countries are developed (mostly Western) while others are developing (mostly non-Western). As criteria for development the UN uses per capita gross domestic products (GDP), share of manufacturing in total GDP, adult literacy rate, augmented quality of life index, economic diversification index, and population size. This classification has implications for the prevalent factors responsible for death and dying in different countries.

2. Western developed nations are different from non-Western developing societies in beliefs and values affecting death and dying practices. Western nations are more individualistic whereas non-Western societies are more collectivistic.

3. The triarchical model explains the environmental dimensions of non-Western developing societies as not being monolithic. The *Global* dimension is universal whereby death is due to biological declines and is expected later as opposed to early in life. Globally, a child's death is considered untimely. Also, sadness following a loss is a universal reaction and is biologically wired. The *Western (developed)* dimension is Westernization influences on non-Western developing societies, including Western medicine and technology in death and dying practices (e.g., embalming, living will, organ donation).

The *non-Western (developed)* dimension is the traditional practices of the indigenous people that persists in the face of Westernization (e.g., beliefs about witchcraft or evil eye as cause of death). Accommodation behavior is maintaining both Western and non-Western beliefs and practices (e.g., accept Western medical cause for death and also traditional beliefs about death causation).

Key Terms

Collectivism
Death culture
Non-Western developing world
Individualism
Triarchical dimensions
Verbal autopsy
Western developed world

Review Questions

1. What are the challenges in having a universal definition for death?
2. What is accommodation behavior?
3. What are examples that reflect collectivism and individualism in death and dying practices?
4. Why do traditional beliefs and practices persist in the face of Westernization influences among non-Westerner?
5. Discuss cultural factors that help to differentiate between Western developed societies from non-Western developing societies.
6. What is group self-esteem and how might this affect the Western definition of personality?
7. If you are a grief counselor or a healthcare practitioner, how might the concept of collectivism and individualism influence your practice with clients from diverse cultures?

Additional Readings

Gardiner, H. W., Gardiner, H., & Kosmitzki, C. (2017). *Lives across cultures: cross-cultural human development.* New York, NY: Pearson's Publishing.

Chapter 2

FRAMEWORKS FOR
BEREAVEMENT AND STRESS

Chapter Outline

Learning objectives
Bereavement models
Grief work
The Four tasks of mourning
Continuing bond with the deceased
Ancestor worship
The dual process model
Meaning reconstruction
Cognitive dissonance
Attribution
Optimism versus pessimism
Intuitive versus instrumental griever
Disenfranchised grief
Complicated or prolonged grief disorder
Nature of stress and coping responses
Pre-dispositional factors and bereavement experience
Stereotype threat and bereavement stress
Bereavement models and perception of stress
Effects of stress on health
Biological reactions to stress
Coping with stress
Predisposition to stress
Influence of social learning on stress perception
Learning by observation or modeling

Learning to connect behavior with consequence
Development of learned helplessness
Explanatory styles
CDC's recommendations for coping with stress
Summary
Key terms
Additional readings

Learning Objectives

LO1: Understand theories and models of bereavement
LO2: Understand the differences between normal and complicated grief
LO3: Describe stress and coping responses
LO4: Understand pre-dispositional factors that influence the perception of stress

Over time different theories and models have been proposed on bereavement and stress, from studies largely conducted on Western populations and the developed world. Some theories and models are descriptive (what to expect as normal or abnormal behaviors) while others are prescriptive (actions to take unto recovery). In addition, some models and theories are stage based (or developmental) whereas others are heuristic (individually paced).

BEREAVEMENT MODELS

Bereavement models have evolved over the years and include the following:

Grief Work

Freud's (1952) model suggests that in order to make a recovery, the bereaved person should actively make efforts to break ties with the deceased. It is counter-intuitive to hold on to the deceased while trying to make a recovery. However, Freud might have thought differently about permanently detaching from the deceased after the loss of his daughter (e.g., Davis, 2004; Rando, 1995).

Four Tasks of Mourning

William Worden's (2008) model expands on Freud's grief work by suggesting that the bereaved should attend to four tasks, but to not break away from the deceased entirely. To acknowledge the loss is the first task (e.g., attend the funeral and/or view the dead body); to feel the pain of the loss is the second task (e.g., cry, deny yourself of some pleasures); to replace the role(s) of the deceased is the third task (e.g., becoming the breadwinner to replace lost income); and to memorialize the deceased and move on with life is the fourth task (e.g., find a way to memorialize or remember the deceased while moving on and forming new relationships). Worden's last stage deviates from Freud's initial approach of severing ties with the deceased.

Continuing Bond with the Desceased

Klass, Silverman, and Nickman's (1996) continuing bond approach is an expansion of maintaining ties with the deceased (e.g., writing letters to the deceased), as a healthy way of moving on, for some individuals. In other words, it is healthy to not let go of the deceased, and it does not signify poor coping and failure to accept the reality of the loss.

Ancestor Worship

Ancestor worship is a type of religion that is popular in non-Western cultures. Ties are maintained with ancestors as a form of continuing bond. However, such ties may be borne out of *necessity* and/or fear of repercussions for failing to do so. It may not necessarily be out of love for the deceased or is made voluntarily because in the afterlife the deceased is believed to have supernatural powers to provide protection and/or bring about good or bad fortunes on the living.

The Dual Process Model

Margaret Stroebe and Schut's (1999) model takes an opposite view to the stage approach in coping with bereavement, suggesting that bereaved persons oscillate between attending to the loss (e.g., feeling the anguish of the loss or "loss orientation") and responding to the new reality created by the loss (e.g., assuming new roles or "restoration orientation"). Progress may be measured when less time is spent focusing on the loss than responding to the new environment created by the loss. However, some people respond to the new environment created by the loss at the expense of not attending to the loss out of expediency e.g., trying to be strong for others while holding own grief reaction in check.

Meaning Reconstruction

Robert Neimeyer's (2001) Meaning reconstruction is said to be the heart of recovery from grief. Several factors could influence Meaning reconstruction including:

Cognitive Dissonance

The meaning you attribute to a death may not be consistent with your behavior. If, for example, your 100-year-old grandmother passed away, and you go about telling people that she lived long enough and you are happy she is no more suffering from pain, but cognitively you believe you will miss her presence, her jokes or wisdom, then there would be inconsistencies between your behavior and thoughts. Leon Festinger (1957) suggests that humans tend to have mental inconsistency with their behavior. In other words, they think one way but act another, and this could create psychological stress or cognitive dissonance, which may not be helpful in the grieving process. Therefore, to reduce cognitive dissonance or psychological stress you need to: a) change your behavior to match the way you think; b) change the way you think to align with your behavior; or) form new ways of thinking e.g., death awaits everyone either sooner or later.

Attribution

Fritz Heider's (1958) Attribution theory describes the process for explaining one's own behavior and that of others, using *Dispositional cause* or *Situational cause*. With dispositional cause, we would attribute death causation to the action of self (e.g., the person died doing what they loved), whereas in situational cause we would attribute death as caused by the action of others (e.g., the person died from another person's recklessness). Based on attributional causes, grief trajectories are going to be different. For example, believers and practitioners of the Islamic religion attribute the cause of death to Allah (God), and not to self because the giver and taker of life is Allah. With such attribution, following a loss the intensity of grief may be reduced or quickly resolved.

Optimism versus Pessimism

Generally, people have a mental attitude regarding outcomes, as either favorable or unfavorable. For some people, a loss could provide opportunities for growth and they embrace it, whereas for others the opportunity of taking on new roles are ignored, while continuing to hold on to the loss. Candice Lightner found opportunities to grow from her loss through Mothers Against Drunk Driving (MADD) which she established in 1980, after she lost her 13-year-old daughter to a drunk driver. MADD provides services to victims and resources for alcohol safety.

Intuitive versus Instrumental Griever

Researcher Kenneth Doka and colleague, Terry Martin (2011) suggest that there are two types of grievers. The *intuitive* griever is more emotional in expression whereas the *instrumental* griever is more cognitive (and tries to master the loss). In some societies, the female is encouraged to be an intuitive griever whereas the male the instrumental griever. It doesn't have to be gender specific, however, as a female may be forced to cognitively master the loss by seizing on growth opportunities such as taking up roles left by a departed spouse as single parent, e.g., seeking paid employment. A male, on the other hand, may be an intuitive griever even when not expressing his emotions outwardly and trying to be strong for family members. Thus, a male griever may look cheerful on the outside but feel sad on the inside.

Disenfranchised Grief

Kenneth Doka (1987) identified grievers whose losses are not acknowledged by society as experiencing disenfranchised grief e.g., grieving the loss from a miscarriage. Thus, the griever's loss becomes a subjective experience that is not shared by everyone. In acknowledging what constitutes a loss, therefore, society may end up disenfranchising some grievers. In the same token, work organizations may stifle grief in not recognizing certain losses by extending paid bereavement leave, e.g., loss of a pet (Eyetsemitan, 1998).

Figure 2.1
Symptoms of "Normal" Versus "Complicated" Grief Reactions (e.g., Shear, 2012).

Normal grief reaction	*Complicated grief reaction*
Recurrent strong feelings to be with the deceased	Continuously ruminating about the circumstance of the death
Deep sorrow and remorse	Continuously worrying about the consequences of the loss and what the future holds in the absence of the deceased
Steady streams of thoughts of the deceased	Unable to find meaning to the loss
Struggle to accept the reality of death of the deceased	Excessively avoiding remainders of the loss
Somatic distress such as digestive symptoms, loss of appetite, fatigue, difficulty initiating or maintaining organized activities	

Source: Shear, K.M. (2012): Grief and mourning gone awry: pathway and course of complicated grief. *Dialogues in Clinical Neuroscience, 14*(2), 119–128.

Complicated or Prolonged Grief Disorder

Grief that is recurring and does not go away becomes complicated grief. About 7% of the US population experience complicated grief (e.g., Kersting et al., 2011). Figure 2.1 illustrates the differences in symptoms between normal and complicated grief reactions.

NATURE OF STRESS AND COPING RESPONSES

Hans Selye (1973) who coined the word *stress* defined it as the demand for change that the body is forced to respond to. As discussed earlier, bereavement could demand change in a person and, therefore, it becomes a stressor. Bereavement could demand change to sleeping patterns, in taking on new responsibilities, in emotional reactions and cognitive reappraisals after a loss (e.g., Hamilton et al., 2016). However, as a stressor bereavement could be perceived as either a *challenge* or a *threat*. As a challenge the reaction to bereavement stress would be

Figure 2.2
Reaction to Bereavement Stress as Threat or Challenge

Characteristic reactions to bereavement stress when perceived as a challenge	*Characteristic reactions to bereavement stress when perceived as a threat*
Making sense of the loss (e.g., Neimeyer & Sands, 2011)	Bitterness and anger (e.g., Shear et al., 2005)
Finding benefits from the loss e.g., becoming more empathetic or forgiving. Experiencing a post-traumatic growth (e.g., Hall, 2011)	Recurring pangs of painful emotions (e.g., Shear et al., 2005)
Seeking secondary resources e.g., social support	Intense yearning and longing for the departed one (e.g., Shear et al., 2005)
Pursuing a new cause or career e.g., becoming an advocate for a cure for cancer	Intrusive and distressing thoughts about the deceased's death (e.g., Shear et al., 2005)
Pursuing actions perceived as pleasing to the deceased e.g., completing a college degree or getting married.	Refusing to provide meaning to or growing from the loss (e.g., Neimeyer & Sands, 2011)

Source: Author's creation

different than if perceived as a threat. As a challenge the bereavement experience could make some individuals to take on new responsibilities such as becoming the bread winner or taking care of younger siblings after a loss. As a threat, however, the bereavement experience may overwhelm the individual, and could lead to withdrawn behavior or depression.

Pre-dispositional Factors and Bereavement Experience

Certain pre-dispositional factors could influence the perception of bereavement stress, as either a challenge or a threat. Such include dependency on the deceased prior to death, and expectations of and preparations for the loss. The more the survivor is dependent on the deceased prior to death the more likely the bereavement experience will be perceived as a threat. Also, a survivor may perceive the bereavement experience as a threat, if the loss was not prepared for nor expected (e.g., Bonanno et al., 2002). In addition, if the loss is not acknowledged by society (e.g., a miscarriage) the bereavement experience may be perceived as a threat (e.g., Doka, 2002). An example of a grief not acknowledged occurred during the funeral of a young man who took his life. The officiating priest condemned the suicide behavior as an ungodly act, not approved by Catholic beliefs. The parents of the young man sued the priest and the church for causing emotional harm (e.g., Rodriguez, 2019, November 20: https://www.usatoday.com/story/news/nation/2019/11/20/michigan-mom-sues-priest-condemning-sons-suicide-funeral/4246968002/).

Stereotype Threat and Bereavement Stress

Stereotype threat occurs when a person's poor performance, behavior or thought patterns conform to negative societal expectations (e.g., Steele et al., 2002). It is usually an affliction of members of a group who are stereotyped in society. If people are aware that their loss is not approved by society, they may experience stereotype threat in their bereavement outcomes. The bereavement stress could be perceived as a threat, resulting in depression.

Bereavement Models and Perception of Stress

The dual process model suggests that bereaved persons oscillate between attending to their loss and responding to the new environment created by their loss (e.g., Stroebe & Schut, 1999). Bereaved individuals who perceive their loss as a threat would devote more time dwelling on the loss than those who perceive it as a challenge. As mentioned earlier, the Four Tasks of Mourning include: 1) accepting the reality of the loss; 2) attending to the pain of the loss; 3) adjusting to the new world without the deceased; and 4) memorializing the deceased while forging ahead with new relationships (e.g., Worden, 2008). When bereavement stress is perceived as a threat, the bereaved is likely to spend more time on stages 1 and 2; as opposed to when perceived as a challenge, he or she would devote more time to stages 3 and 4 (and possibly grow from the loss). The meaning ascribed to a loss (Neimeyer & Sands, 2011) and/or explanatory styles for a loss, could also lead to bereavement stress being perceived as either a threat or a challenge. When the survivor cannot find a satisfactory meaning to a loss as in the case of the loss of a child or suicide, bereavement stress could be perceived as a threat and could result in an unhealthy continuing bond with the deceased (e.g., Klass et al., 1996; Neimeyer, 2001).

Effects of Stress on Health

Stress could result in sleep disturbances, irritability, or poor immunity. Also, it could negatively impact on a person's mental health (e.g., depression, anxiety disorder), leading to PTSD (post-traumatic stress disorder) and personality disorders such as psychosis (e.g., Kay & Tasman, 2006). Stress also could give rise to cardiovascular diseases (e.g., Iso, Date, Yamamoto et al., 2002), obesity (e.g., Dallman, Pecoraro, Akana et al., 2003), respiratory impairment (e.g., Lehrer et al., 2006), and tumor growth (e.g., Antoni, Lutgendorf, Cole et al., 2006). Stress also can damage a person's DNA resulting in a shortened *telomere* (a structure the end of the chromosome), which could reduce life expectancy. However, having sustained stress is more likely to cause damage to a person's telomeres (e.g., Mathur et al., 2016).

Biological Reactions to Stress

Biological theories suggest that the human body has a "fight or flight" response to stress (e.g., Rom & Reznick, 2015). The body is mobilized to either confront or avoid a stressful situation. Biological reactions to the news about an unexpected loss could result in the pounding of the chest, dry mouth, or tense muscle. If this reaction is sustained over time, the result could be high blood pressure, induce artery-clogging deposits, and disturbed sleep patterns; also anxiety, depression, obesity, addiction and death (e.g., Harvard Health Publishing, 2018, May 1; https://www.health.harvard.edu/staying-healthy/understanding-the-stress-response).

COPING WITH STRESS

The ability to cope with stress is influenced by several factors including personality disposition, previous experience with stress, cognitive evaluation of the stressful event, and available resources.

Predisposition to Stress

The following predisposing factors could influence a person's ability to cope with stress:

- Oversensitivity to a particular stressful situation resulting in stress being perceived as a threat (e.g., Bilikiewicz, Puzynski, Rybakowski, & Wiórka 2002).
- A tendency toward depression or mental disorder (e.g., anxiety) could result in the manifestation of that illness, if exposed to a stressful situation (e.g., Dantzer, O'Connor & Fruend, et al, 2008).
- Prior learning such as pessimism could result in stress being perceived as a threat.

Influence of Social Learning on Stress Perception

Social learning can influence how you respond to a stressful situation. Social learning provides a cognitive framework or a perceptual set for evaluating a situation as being stressful or not, as a threat or a challenge. The following models exemplify social learning and stress perception as a threat or a challenge:

Learning by Observation or Modeling

Albert Bandura and Richard Walters (1977) propose that through observation or modeling people can learn positive or negative behaviors by imitating, observing, or modeling the actions of others such as a parent, a teacher or a clergy. However, the learner has to be attentive, be able to store information in memory, and be motivated to repeat what has been learned.

How role models handle their stressful situations could become a template for how others would handle theirs in the future. Did the role model cry, avoid calling the deceased by name, avoid talking about the deceased or avoid reminders of the deceased such as putting photos away? In the advent of a loss, adults try to remain "strong" for young children and they try to not display their true emotions. However, following a loss changes in the child's environment such as lost opportunities or not being able to continue with schooling could affect the child's perception of bereavement stress as a threat. For older children, however, lost opportunities resulting from bereavement, might provide room for growth through taking on of new roles and responsibilities. Generally, young children are better able to cope with stress arising from a loss if normalcy is restored as best possible in their daily routine.

Learning to Connect Behavior with Consequence

Psychologist B. F. Skinner's (1938) operant conditioning theory states that based on reward or punishment a behavior is either reinforced or not reinforced in the future. Thus, a person learns to make a connection between a behavior and its consequence. A survivor's expression of pain and grief following a loss, can either be acknowledged or not, by others. Thus, with available social support following a loss the survivor could perceive bereavement stress as less of a threat.

Development of Learned Helplessness

Psychologist Martin Seligman (1975) in his book entitled, *Helplessness: On Depression, Development, and Death* suggests that a lack of control or poor self-efficacy (a lack of belief in one's capacity to do things) is derived from learned helplessness. When a person's repeated actions are not rewarded, over time he or she develops learned helplessness (stopping to try to change their situation). Due to learned helplessness, a person is likely to perceive bereavement stress as a threat and may fail to take actions to cope with the stress.

Explanatory Styles

The attribution a person makes to life events can affect how bereavement stress is perceived. As stated earlier, Attributions could be positive or negative and could be made either to self or to a situation (e.g., Kassin, Fein & Marcus, 2013). An example of an attribution made to self is blaming oneself for the loss of a loved one, which is negative. This could lead to the perception of bereavement stress as a threat. However, a positive attribution to self would be the satisfaction with efforts made to prevent a loved one's death e.g., helping to provide for a good medical care. Such an attribution would lead to the perception of bereavement stress as a challenge, instead. Also, death from lung cancer attributed to the deceased person's smoking habit, may result in the personal growth in values by the survivors. Jason Horowitz (2016; New York Times; https://www.nytimes.com/2016 /01/03/us/politics/for-donald-trump-lessons-from-a-brothers-suffering .html) reported that President Donald Trump's older brother, Freddy (junior), died from alcohol addiction in 1981 at the age of 43, and his death had a lasting impact on the president in choosing to avoid alcohol or cigarette use thereafter.

CDC's RECOMMENDATIONS FOR COPING WITH STRESS

The Center for Disease Control recommends the following as measures for coping with stress (CDC, cdc.gov; https://www.cdc.gov /violenceprevention/suicide/copingwith-stresstips.html):

- Exercise: The release of endorphins (a type of hormone) makes you feel better and improves your immune system.
- Eat well-balanced and healthy meals. Some people have the tendency to find solace in food when under stress.
- Rest enables the body to repair and recover, so get plenty of sleep.
- Share your burden with others—friend, parent, counselor, doctor, or clergy. They may help you appreciate alternative perspectives and help you with meaning reconstruction, also. Women, more than men, take advantage of social support, enabling them to improve on coping effectiveness and in immune functioning (e.g., Hobfoll, Dunahoo, Ben-Porath, & Monnier, 1994).
- Avoid the use of drugs and alcohol: Drugs and alcohol may change the reality of the situation temporarily but could lead to problems of addiction through long term use.
- If having suicidal ideations, talk to a professional such as a counselor, psychologist or social worker.

Whereas each individual manages stress differently, it is important to take into consideration the person's predisposing circumstances and social learning exposure prior to a loss, in helping them cope better with bereavement stress.

SUMMARY

1. There are different models and theories that help to explain bereavement. Some are descriptive (what to expect as normal or abnormal behaviors) while others are prescriptive (what actions to take unto recovery).
2. As a way unto recovery, bereavement models include breaking ties with the deceased; addressing particular tasks of mourning; maintaining continuing bond with the deceased while forming new relationships; oscillating between attending to the loss and the reality of the new world created by the loss; and providing meaning reconstruction to the loss.
3. Stress could accompany a loss, resulting in sleep disturbance, depression, irritability, or poor immunity. It could also impact negatively on a person's mental health (e.g., anxiety disorder, psychosis). It damages a person's DNA, shortening life expectancy, especially when the stress is chronic.
4. Stress could be perceived as a threat or a challenge, with opportunity for growth.
5. Coping with stress is influenced by personality disposition, previous experience with stress, cognitive evaluation of the stressful event and available resources.

Key Terms

Bereaved
Bereavement models
Complicated grief
Coping
Disenfranchised grief
Stress

Review Questions

1. Which bereavement models make better sense to you and why?
2. What type of loss would be a threat to you and why?
3. What type of loss would be a challenge to you and why?
4. What predisposing factors (e.g., cognition, prior learning or prior experience) would enable you to cope or not to cope with a loss?

5. Can you describe the primary resources (e.g., abilities) or secondary resources (e.g., social support) that would enable you to better cope with a loss?

Additional Readings

Anisman, H. (2014). *An introduction to stress and health.* Thousand Oaks, CA: Sage.

Chapter 3

DEATH, DYING AND BEREAVEMENT IN AFRICA

Chapter Outline

Learning objectives
Life expectancy and prevalent causes of death
Beliefs about death and dying
Beliefs about afterlife
Bereavement
Summary
Key words
Review questions
Additional readings

Learning Objectives

LO1: Comprehend the life expectancy differentials of countries in Africa.
LO2: Explain the predominant causes of death in Africa
LO3: Describe death, dying and bereavement practices that reflect Collectivism
LO4: Describe death, dying and bereavement practices that reflect Individualism
LO5: Describe death, dying and bereavement practices that reflect Accommodation behavior.
LO6: Explain African Traditional religious beliefs about the afterlife
LO7: Understand African traditional beliefs about death and dying

Figure 3.1
Map of Africa

Countries of Africa (N=54)

Algeria	Ethiopia	Niger
Angola	Gabon	Nigeria
Benin	Gambia, The	Rwanda
Botswana	Ghana	São Tomé and Príncipe
Burkina Faso	Guinea	Senegal
Burundi	Guinea-Bissau	Seychelles
Cameroon	Kenya	Sierra Leone
Cape Verde	Lesotho	Somalia
Central African Republic	Liberia	South Africa
Chad	Liberia	Sudan
Comoros	Lbya	South Sudan
Congo	Madagascar	Swaziland
Congo, Democratic	Malawi	Tanzania
Republic of the	Mali	Togo
Côte d'Ivoire	Mauritania	Tunisia
Djibouti	Mauritius	Uganda
Egypt	Morocco	Zambia
Equatorial Guinea	Mozambique	Zimbabwe
Eritrea	Namibia	

Source: Istockphoto.com

LIFE EXPECTANCY AND PREVALENT CAUSES OF DEATH

In Africa, whereas 14 countries have life expectancy below 60 years, no nation has a life expectancy of 80 years or above. Figures 3.2 and 3.3, respectively, illustrate the top 10 countries with the highest life expectancy and those with the lowest life expectancy.

Figure 3.2
Top 10 Countries with Highest Life Expectancy At Birth in Africa, 2017

Country	Life expectancy at birth (in years)
Morocco	77.10
Algeria	77.00
Libya	76.70
Mauritius	75.80
Tunisia	75.70
Seychelles	74.90
Egypt	73.00
Cabo Verde	72.40
Ghana	67.00
Madagascar	66.30

Source: CIA The World Factbook; https://www.cia.gov/library/publications/the-world -factbook/rankorder/2102rank.html

Figure 3.3
Top 10 Countries with Lowest Life Expectancy in Africa, 2017

Country	Life Expectancy (in years)
Congo	57.70
Burkina Faso	55.90
Uganda	55.90
Niger	55.90
Nigeria	53.80
Mozambique	53.70
Lesotho	53.00
Central African Republic	52.80
Somalia	52.80
Zambia	52.70
Swaziland	52.10
Gabon	52.00
Guinea Bissau	51.00
Chad	50.60

Source: The World Factbook; https://www.cia.gov/library/publications/the-world-fact-book/rankorder/2102rank.html

The World Bank (2020) classifies countries with less than $1,025 Gross National Income per capita as low-income countries; those with between $1,026 and $3,995 as lower middle income countries; those with between $3,996 and $12,375 as upper-middle income countries; and those with incomes of more than $12,376 as high-income countries. Most African countries fall under the low-income category (data-helpdesk.WorldBank.org, 2020). On face value these classifications do point to available resource per capita and insight into a country's human development capacity, especially when factored in with population density.

Figures 3.2 and 3.3 show that only eight countries have life expectancy above 70 years, implying that most deaths occur within a contracted age range. As shown later, in the top 10 leading causes of death in Africa are deaths that occur in childhood, including preterm birth complications and birth asphyxia and birth trauma. Also the top two, lower respiratory diseases and diarrheal infections, are the leading causes of death among children in lower income countries (e.g., Black, Morris & Bryce, 2003).

Also, the variation between the highest life expectancy of 77.10 years (for Morocco) and the lowest of 50.60 years (for Chad) is over 25 years, indicating a lopsided human capital development capacity across the continent. According to WHO (2018; https://www.who.int /news-room/fact-sheets/detail/the-top-10-causes-of-death) in low income economies (which the majority of African countries fall under in 2016), the top 10 leading causes of death include:

1. Lower respiratory disease
2. Diarrheal diseases
3. Ischaemic heart disease
4. HIV/AIDS
5. Stroke
6. Malaria
7. Tuberculosis
8. Preterm birth complications
9. Birth asphyxia and birth trauma
10. Road injury

Source: WHO (2018; https://www.who.int/news-room/fact-sheets/detail/the-top-10-causes-of-death).

BELIEFS ABOUT DEATH AND DYING

In Africa, as with most collectivist cultures, the socialization process places group needs over individual needs; making, for example, medical care decisions be group based rather than the individual's preference (e.g., Lanre-Abass, 2008). That aside, Africans would prefer life-sustaining treatments to personal measures to end life such as physician-assisted suicide or euthanasia (e.g., Onukwugha & Alfandre, 2019). Usually, death is attributed to evil forces or witchcraft, especially when Western medicine fails to provide a cure for disease. Sub-

Saharan Africa has the highest infant mortality rate in the world (UNICEF, 2019; https://data.unicef.org/topic/child-survival/under-five-mortality/). Yet, death in childhood just as with every other society, is regarded as untimely. In rural areas, measures taken to prevent premature death in children are more spiritual, due to belief systems and poor medical facilities. Such preventive measures include the prayers by a traditional priest or getting the child to wear a necklace of amulets prepared by traditional healers, to forestall the wicked acts of witches. In urban settings, belief in spiritual rather than in medical remedies is pervasive also, due to rural-urban migration.

Road traffic accident is included in the top 10 causes of death in many countries of Africa (WHO, 2020; https://www.who.int/newsroom /fact-sheets/detail/road-traffic-injuries). Instead of obeying traffic rules and ensuring that their vehicles are road worthy, operators of public transport rely on good luck charms prepared by traditional healers to prevent accidents. Lesiba Baloyi (2009: http://uir.unisa.ac .za/handle /10500/1346) notes that in untimely deaths medical malpractice is excused, because of belief in evil forces, witchcraft, or evil acts of a wicked neighbor. Schmidt-Leukel (2006) also notes the extent of beliefs in evil forces, thus: *"Evil spirits or witches may also cause death against God's intentions. Especially people who die at a young age or under strange circumstances are considered to be killed by evil forces"* (p. 41)

BELIEFS ABOUT AFTERLIFE

African traditional religion, unlike Christian teachings and beliefs, does not believe in heaven nor hell, in the afterlife. The deceased person however is believed to exist in spirit form with other ancestors in an otherworld (e.g., Nobles, 2006). If a person dies in old age he or she becomes an Ancestor, who continues to provide protection and guidance for loved ones, with supernatural abilities. Deceased children are not considered as Ancestors because of their young age. While alive children are not in a position to provide protection and guidance to loved ones and could not do so in the afterlife. The roles in which children function in the afterlife is not clearly defined, as in the Islamic religion which would be discussed in a later chapter. Ancestors are worshipped, venerated, and respected by loved ones (e.g., King, 2013), which is not conceivable for young children.

There is an active engagement of the living with the "living" dead, whose name is invoked at important family and community events, for blessings and protection. During merriments Ancestors are not left out, either. In festive occasions they are first to be served drinks or *libation* that is poured on the floor/ground indicating the ancestor's abode as earth burial remains the preferred mode of burial. The drink offering that is first made to the Ancestors is to seek their blessings so that the activities would go on smoothly.

In African traditional religion beliefs in reincarnation is different than that professed in Hinduism or Buddhism. Ancestors are believed to return to earth to complete the cycle of life in another human form, but as children in their original families. Genetics apart, the physical resemblance of a newborn child to a departed Ancestor, especially if the child's gender matches that of the Ancestor's, helps to reinforce this belief. For example, among Nigeria's Yoruba ethnic group such names as Iyabo (meaning mother is back) is common among females. Also, Babajide (father awoke from the dead) is also common among males.

As already explained, a child's death may be the result of childbirth, medical or public health issues. In the African traditional belief system, however, the death of a child is perceived differently; it could be seen as the wrath of an ancestor punishing the living (e.g., Maboea, 2002). When infants come into the world and die soon after, they are believed to be "spirit children" who only came to torment their parents. The Yoruba of Nigeria call such children *Abiku* (meaning born to die) and the Ibos, another Nigerian ethnic group, call them *Ogbanje* (meaning a spirit that deliberately accurses a family with evil). Tokunbo Adeyemo (1979) suggests that in death two worlds are separated: the worlds of the living and of the spirits; and it is by appeasing the ancestors that both worlds can be reconciled.

Also, African traditional religious belief system runs contrary to Islamic teachings about the afterlife. Yet there is a large following of believers in the Christian and Islamic faiths in Africa. In Sub-Saharan Africa, Christians are projected to grow from 517 million in 2010 to 1.1 billion in 2050, and the Muslim population is expected to rise from 248 million to 670 million within that same period (e.g., Pewforum.org; 2015: https://www.pewforum.org/2015/04/02/sub-saharan-africa/).

In a Pew Research Center (2010b) study (https://www.pewforum .org/2010/04/15/executive-summary-islam-and-christianity-in-sub

-saharan-africa/) adherents of both religions indicate that they believe in heaven and hell, in the teachings of the Bible or the Koran, and that they participate in weekly worship services; and that they pray once a day (or 5 times a day in the case of Muslims). Yet, African traditional religious practices still persists among followers of both faiths. There are over 100 million African traditional religion practitioners spread across 45 countries in the continent (e.g., Lugira, 2009). As discussed in Chapter 1, the environment of Africa is not monolithic and is made up of a triarchical dimension, resulting in people adhering to both Western and non-Western belief systems and exemplifying "accommodation" behavior (e.g., Gottlieb, 2006).

BEREAVEMENT

The triarchical environmental dimensions of Global, Western and non-Western are influential in the bereavement process following a loss. In the global dimension, the emotion of sadness follows a loss, especially if the death is unexpected. The loss of a child is of a particularly painful event, as customarily parents are not expected to bury their children; rather the opposite should be the case. Sadness is a basic emotion shared by all humans (e.g., Black & Yacoob, 1997). While facial expressions help to indicate sadness, however, the actions or words said also indicate our emotional state. Thus, in Africa behaviors such as crying, denying oneself of daily pleasures, wearing of black clothes, or shaving of one's hair are ways of expressing sadness during bereavement.

Generally, Western influences on African belief systems about the afterlife, is influenced by Christian teachings. The deceased is believed to go to heaven or hell or purgatory (in Catholic theology). Christian funerals would include a church service, officiated by a priest or minister. In Christian teachings, God determines the location of the deceased in the afterlife, after judgment. People who lived a righteous life but more importantly accepted Christ as savior prior to death go to heaven as a reward. Hell, as punishment, is reserved for people who did not live a righteous life and more importantly did not accept Christ as savior, prior to death. The Bible in 2 Thessalonians 1:9-10 states that: *"They shall suffer the punishment of eternal destruction and exclusion from the presence of the Lord and from the glory of his might, when he comes on that day to be glorified by his saints."*

Unlike Ancestor worship, Christian teachings do not include reincarnation after death. Christian funerals are meant to celebrate the deceased, if she or he led a Christian life and accepted Christ as savior prior to death. Words such as "home going" are commonly used, indicative of a positive outcome for death. In Christian theology, it is more important to die young and go to heaven or "home," than to live a long life and die and go to hell. Usually, committal service at the graveside would have the priest or minister read from the scripture and say words such as: "We therefore commit (his or her) body to the ground; earth to earth, ashes to ashes, dust to dust; in the sure and certain hope of the Resurrection to eternal life." (BBC, 2009: Christian funerals; https://www.bbc.co.uk/religion/religions/christianity/rites rituals/funerals.shtml)

In the non-Western system of thought, death before old age is seen as a disruption of the normal course of life brought about by evil spirits or sorcery, even if medical evidence suggests that the cause of death is due to an infectious disease (diarrheal infection or COVID-19). Therefore, bereavement begins by first seeking the spiritual cause of death from a traditional healer and by listening to prescriptions on how to prevent similar deaths from happening to family members in the future. This might require traditional rituals (e.g., Smith, 1974). Usually, burial is conducted in the ancestral land of the deceased, possibly in the ancestral home where the spirit of the deceased can join those of the ancestors. Occasionally when burials take place in foreign lands for practical reasons, pieces of the decedent's body such as hair, toe nails or finger nails are brought back to the Ancestral land for burial, believing that the deceased's spirit has now joined its forebears. Among the Ashantis of Ghana, burial rituals also include the offering of sacrifices on behalf of the deceased in the ancestral land; in appeasement to the Ancestors whom the deceased would soon become a part of (e.g., van der Geest, 2000). These are proactive measures to ensure that no harm would be brought on the living by the "living dead."

As earlier discussed, as an expression of sadness the grieving process includes the shaving of hair and wearing of black clothes, to symbolize the dark cloud that death has brought about. This outward expression of grief enables a stranger to be respectful of what the mourner is experiencing and to offer whatever assistance he or she is able to give. Bereavement rituals also place behavioral restrictions on the mourner such as avoiding the pleasures of life e.g., going to a movie or a ball game. For example, the Bapedi of South Africa forbids a widow from arriving home after sunset or a widower from having intimate relationships before a set time period, usually between six months to one year. Such observances are believed in helping to restore harmony to the disruption caused by death (e.g., Baloyi, 2009).

After the mourning period, there is an elaborate celebration and the mourner stops to wear black clothes. In Kenya the Abanyala (a sub-group of the Abaluhya) celebrate the end of the mourning period by slaughtering and eating chickens and cows. In Uganda, the Buganda tribe call the post-bereavement celebration "destroying death" (Okwaabya olumbe), and male survivors gather at the home of the deceased to eat chicken (e.g., Ray, 1980).

As discussed earlier, many Africans profess Christianity or Islam but also engage in Ancestor worship, which holds a different belief system about the afterlife. Thus, many Africans exhibit accommodation behavior. Ancestor worship is not just a religion but also a cultural identity. Thus, Christian identity does no replace ethnic group identity, which could explain for accommodation behavior. For example, in ceremonies to recognize the accomplishments of deserving ethnic group members (who are Christians), rituals akin to Ancestor worship, including libation to ancestors to bless the event are also performed. According to Harry Triandis (1995), in collectivist cultures, the individual's goals are subsumed within the fabric of the in-group's goals.

SUMMARY

1. Most African profess Christianity, Islam and/or Ancestor worship (Traditional African religion). Unlike Christianity or Islam, Ancestor worshippers believe in reincarnation.
2. Many Africans are dual practitioners of a foreign religion (e.g., Christianity or Islam) and Traditional indigenous religion of Ancestor worship (including spiritual beliefs for death causation). This is an indication of accommodation behavior.
3. Many Africans have a self-identity subsumed within the in-group and beliefs are based on collectivistic values.
4. In Africa the prevalent causes of death are communicable diseases. Prominent causes of death in childhood include maternal, neonatal, and nutritional factors.

Key Terms

Accommodation behavior
African Traditional religious beliefs
Ancestor worship
Christianity
Islam
Sorcery
Spirit
Spirit children
Witchcraft

Review Questions

1. What would be examples of how Africans exemplify accommodation behavior?
2. What are African Traditional religious beliefs about the Afterlife?
3. Why do African Traditional religious beliefs persist in the face of foreign religious influences?
4. How do beliefs in witchcraft and sorcery likely to influence health seeking behavior or preventive measures against traffic accidents?
5. Can a dual belief in Christianity and African traditional religion complicate bereavement?

Additional Readings

Adogame, A., Chitando, E., & Bateye, B. (Eds) (2016). *African traditions in the study of religions in Africa.* Abingdon, UK: Routledge
Eyetsemitan, F. (2002). Cultural interpretation of dying and death in a non-western society: The case of Nigeria. Online Readings in Psychology and Culture-q -scholarworks.gvsu.edu
Golomski, C. (2018). *Funeral culture: AIDS, work and culture change in an African kingdom.* Bloomington, IN: Indiana University Press.

Chapter 4

DEATH, DYING AND BEREAVEMENT IN THE MIDDLE EAST

Chapter Outline

Learning objectives
Life expectancy and the prevalent causes of death
Death attitudes
Influence of religious beliefs on grief models
Death and dying practices in Israel
Key words
Summary
Review questions
Additional readings

Learning Objectives

LO1: Understand the predominant causes of death among the peoples of the Middle East region

LO2: Explain death, dying and bereavement practices and belief systems of peoples of the Middle East region that reflect on collectivism

LO3: Explain death, dying and bereavement practices and belief systems of peoples of the Middle East region that reflect on individualism

LO4: Examine death, dying and bereavement prractices and beliefs that reflect on Accommodation behavior

LO5: Explain Islam's predominant impact on death attitude and death socialization

41

LO6: Identify challenges to Westernization influences on death, dying and bereavement practices in the Middle East region

LO7: Compare and contrast Judaism and Islam on death and dying beliefs and practices

Figure 4.1
Map of The Middle East Region

Source: Istockphoto.com

LIFE EXPECTANCY AND PREVALENT CAUSES OF DEATH

In Figure 4.2, of the 15 countries listed two have life expectancy of 80 years and above, but most are in the age range of 70 years, except for Yemen which is below 70 years. The leading causes of death for most the countries in the region are communicable diseases.

Figure 4.2
Life Expectancy of Countries in the Middle East Estimated at Birth, 2017

Country	Life Expectancy (in years)
Israel	82.50
Malta	80.50
Lebanon	77.80
Quatar	78.90
Bahrain	79.00
Oman	75.70
United Arab Emirates	77.70
Iran	74.00
Kuwait	78.20
Saudi Arabia	75.50
Jordan	74.80
West bank and Gaza	74.20
Syria	75.10
Iraq	74.90
Yemen	65.90

Source: CIA: The World Factbook; https://www.cia.gov/library/publications/the-world-factbook/rankorder/2102rank.html

As indicated in the previous chapter, the World Bank (2020) classifies nations with less than $1,025 Gross National Income per capita as low-income countries, countries with between $1,026 and $3,995 as lower-middle income societies, those between $3,996 and $12,375 as upper-middle income countries, and nations with incomes of more than $12,376 as high-income countries (e.g., datahelpdesk.WorldBank.org, 2020). The high-income countries include Bahrain, Israel, Malta, Oman, Qatar, United Arab Emirates, Kuwait and Saudi Arabia. The rest are either low-income or middle-income countries. The WHO (2018; https://www.who.int/news-room/fact-sheets/detail/the-top-10 -causes-of-death) lists the 10 leading causes of death in high income countries (which a slight majority of the countries fall under) in 2016 as:

1. Ischaemic heart disease
2. Stroke
3. Alzheimer disease
4. Trachea, bronchus, lung cancers
5. Chronic obstructive pulmonary disease
6. Lower respiratory infection
7. Colon and rectum cancers
8. Diabetes melitus
9. Kidney disease
10. Breast cancer

Aside lower respiratory infection (a communicable condition), the rest of the factors are non-communicable, thereby helping to reduce the spread of death-causing contagions.

DEATH ATTITUDES

Most Middle Eastern countries are non-Western societies, but they are also influenced by the global, Western, and non-Western factors as discussed in previous chapters. As earlier mentioned, a global factor following a loss is a universal emotion. Sadness is not just a facial display but is also in behaviors that are culturally sanctioned. Islam, being the predominant religion in the Middle East, is influential in the socialization of bereavement practices. In the Islamic teachings, the behavioral display of sadness following a loss would be muted because the religion teaches a total submission to the will of Allah (God), even in unexpected death (e.g., Kristiansen & Sheikh,, 2012). In Arabic, Islam means to "surrender" (Britannica.com, https://www .britannica.com/topic/Islam; n.d.). However, sadness could be experienced without an outward display, especially in the loss of a child, which goes against conventional understanding in most societies.

Most scholars agree that Islam originated in the Middle East in Mecca and Medina of Saudi Arabia (e.g., Watt, 2014). According to the Pew Research Center (2017: https://www.pewresearch.org/fact-tank/2017/01/31/worlds-muslim-population-more-widespread-than-you-might-think/) the Middle East (including North Africa) has the highest concentration of Muslims of any region of the world. Islam constitutes 93% of the region's 341 million inhabitants. Islam not only teaches on the relationship between the individual and God, but also on how people should act in social situations. Thus, in the region Islamic laws (Sharia) that prescribe how society should be governed are enacted (e.g., Britannica.com, n.d.; https://www.britannica.com /topic/Islam).

Islam teaches that God who created man can also cause him to die, and that death cannot happen except by God's will. Therefore, through a lifestyle prescribed by Islam, adherents of the faith should enjoy a life of "peace" no matter their circumstance (Britannica.com, n.d.; https://www.britannica.com/topic/Islam/). Death rituals are not elaborate and include washing of the dead body (ablusion), wrapping of the dead body with white cloth, and burial of the deceased before sunset. Earth burial is prescribed, with no embalming required, and other forms of burial is shunned, including cremation and above-ground mausoleum (e.g., Mehraby, 2003). Also, the use of casket is avoided because it comes between the body and the earth to which the deceased must return. The deceased's face is made to turn toward the East (that is Mecca), symbolizing a state of prayer. Burial ceremony would include the customary saying of words on the submissive teachings of Islam which is absolute trust in God as giver and taker of life (Mehraby, 2003).

Islamic teachings being the dominant practice in the Middle East, Westernization influences might have to adapt to the prevailing culture (e.g., Baider & Goldzweig, 2016). Saudi physician Mohammad Zafir Al-Shahri (2002) notes that most of the Saudi Arabian healthcare system is staffed by healthcare professionals that are recruited from outside of the country. In meeting the patients' needs which are mainly shaped by the Islamic religion, therefore, the foreign healthcare practitioners would have to make adjustments. Although English is the official language for communication and documentation in the healthcare system, the language has to be used in a manner that is culturally sensitive. Mona El-Kurd (2012; https://www.pcqn.org/wp-content

/uploads/2012/11/Sept-Call_Cultural-Diversity-and-Caring-For
-Patients-From-Middle-East.pdf) notes that in communication between
a patient and a physician, Muslims repeat words to demonstrate the
importance of the matter at hand, and it does not signal that the physician is perceived as having hearing deficits.

Furthermore, a Muslim patient prefers that the physician priori-
tizes context and relationship building over the message itself. Also,
foreign physicians should be sensitive in communicating lifestyle practices that could lead to diseases and death, such as smoking which is
prevalent among males (e.g., Al-Shahri, 2002) and being overweight
due to a lack of exercise which is common among females (e.g., El-
Hazmi & Warsy, 1997). With alcohol use, sexual relations outside of
marriage, and smoking among females as forbidden by the Islamic
religion, communication between a physician and a patient that
touches on such matters should be approached with care and sensitivity. Predestination in Islamic teachings does not prevent Saudis
from seeking Western medical treatment (e.g., Sebai et al., 2001) neither from approaching traditional healers for healing—a form of
accommodation behavior. According to Saudi physician Mahammed
Zafir Al-Shahri (2002), a traditional healer, however, may request that
a patient discontinue Western medical treatment as a condition for
offering assistance. Spiritual healing is another form of healing sub-
scribed to by the Saudis. It is based on the recitation of verses from
the Koran and the specific sayings of the Prophet Mohammed. Spiritual healing is used in particular against the effects of "evil eye" (e.g.,
Qamar, 2013). In both communicating and providing treatment regi-
mens to the Saudi patient, foreign health practitioners should be
aware of all these alternative approaches to healing. In Figure 4.3,
Mona El-Kurd (2012; https://www.pcqn.org/wp-content/uploads
/2012/11/Sept-Call_Cultural-Diversity-and-Caring-For-Patients-From
-Middle-East.pdf) draws attention to the contrast between the cultures
of Western medicine and the cultures of the Middle Eastern people.

Figure 4.3
Contrasts Between the Cultures of Western Medicine
and the Cultures of the Middle Eastern People

Culture of Western medicine	Culture of the Middle Eastern people
Dominance over nature	Reliance on the group in coping with illness
Timeliness—sooner is better than later	Prefer same sex caregivers over a competent caregiver of opposite sex
Aggressive therapy—stronger is better	Bad news should not be given to the patient directly but through an elder in the family
Standardization of treatment is better	Approach to treatment should be cognizance of patient's age and gender
Task oriented	Relationship oriented
Scientific basis for illness	Belief in "evil" eye
Preventive medicine is helpful	Religious beliefs about behaviors that adversely affect health (e.g., smoking) are more important than medical findings
End-of-life decision should be an individual's choice	Euthanasia and Physician-assisted suicide are forbidden

Source: Mona El-Kurd, 2012; https://www.pcqn.org/wp-content/uploads/2012/11/Sept
-Call_Cultural-Diversity-and-Caring-For-Patients-From-Middle-East.pdf

INFLUENCE OF ISLAMIC RELIGIOUS BELIEFS ON GRIEF MODELS

Islamic religious beliefs put to test Worden's (2008) Four tasks of mourning and Elisabeth Kubler Ross' (1969) five stages of dying. In William Worden's (2008) four tasks of mourning, the following are suggested toward a recovery: 1) Accept the Reality of the Loss: The survivor has to come to terms with the reality that the loved one is no more. To the visual senses attending the deceased's funeral might help to confirm this reality; however, the human brain might yet to accept the loss, or even reject it (similar to cognitive dissonance discussed in Chapter 2). Worden does not provide a timeline for this stage. In the case of an unexpected death it might take a relatively longer time to come to terms with the reality of the loss, cognitively. The Islamic belief that God is both the giver and taker of life might help with the acceptance of the loss sooner, even if unexpected. 2) Work through the pain of the loss: With loss comes the reactions of sadness, longingness, emptiness, numbness, and confusion which are normal (e.g., Shear, 2012). The bereaved person should allow the reactions to take their course without holding back. Although the Islamic religion teaches that God determines a person's appointed time of death, the loss creates a void in a confidant, a husband, a brother, or a co-worker who is no more. In the face of a void created by a loss, an open display of sadness, longingness, emptiness or confusion can betray one's faith in God as the giver and taker of life. Furthermore, Muslims may perceive fellow Muslims as showing signs of spiritual weakness and not trusting in Allah, if he or she expresses despair, sadness or anger as a result of a loss (e.g., Worth, Irshad, Bhopal et al., 2009).

While individuals vary in their reactions to a loss, the predictions of denial and anger espoused by Western bereavement models are less common among Muslims (e.g., Sheikh & Gatrad, 2008). For Muslims, death is not a taboo subject (e.g., Kristiansen & Sheikh, 2012). Muslims are encouraged to focus on spiritual growth than on material things and to be mindful of the temporal nature of life. In the loss of a loved one, they are reminded of the transient nature of life which serves to draw them closer to the Creator and to allow for God's mercy (e.g., Ramadan, 2010). 3). Adjust to the new environment created by the loss: Adjustment to a loss may be gradual or immediate and may require much or little time, depending on the impact of the loss on the survivor. Also, adjustment to a loss could be physical, mental, and/or spiritual and may involve taking on new roles and responsibilities or seeking help from others. This reality applies to a survivor, irrespective of the survivor's religious disposition. However, adjustment to a loss is made easier with a large network of social support structure, which is common to collectivist cultures such as the Middle Eastern societies. 4). Memorialize the deceased while moving on with your life: The survivor should look for ways to remember or immortalize the deceased, while getting on with his or her life after the loss, including forming new relationships. How the survivor chooses to memorialize the deceased might be a personal decision. However, in collectivist cultures moving on with life and forming new relationships could be a group decision by the survivor's family e.g., in getting a new spouse for the survivor. However, due to Westernization influences the practice of *arranged marriage* (a marriage in which spouses are chosen for each other by parents and family members) is becoming a thing of the past (e.g., Sabra, 2016; https://www.dandc.eu/en/article/fewer-arranged -marriages-arab-countries).

Certain types of death are atypical, however, including the loss of a young child which goes against the norm of death's timing. Parents do not believe they should bury their children, rather it should be the other way around. The death of a young child is a very distressing experience. Yet the Islamic faith expect parents to find comfort in the child's innocence and that the child has gone to pave the way for the parents to enter Paradise (e.g., Hedayat, 2006). Other difficult losses to grieve include death resulting from un-Islamic behaviors such as drug abuse. A death that is contrary to Islamic teachings could lead to disenfranchised grief due to a lack of societal approval (e.g., Doka, 2002) and to complicated grief outcomes (e.g., Kristiansen & Sheikh, 2012).

During bereavement, in addition to condolence visits, fellow Muslims offer tangible support including preparing of food, running errands, or taking care of young children. The Muslim woman must not remarry until after four months and ten days following her husband's death. This is to ensure that she is not pregnant by her deceased husband. With Westernization influences, advanced technology, however, may help in determining conception before four months and 10 days through a pregnancy test or an early ultrasound scan (e.g., Mehraby, 2003). Irrespective of this, the belief in waiting four months and ten days may supplant the availability of modern technology.

Physician Elizabeth Kubler Ross (1969) identifies five stages that a person goes through in dying: 1) denial, 2) anger, 3) bargaining, 4) depression, and 5) acceptance. The first stage of denial comes after receiving the bad news (of dying) from the physician. Before finally accepting the bad news, however, seeking multiple medical opinions may be involved. The second stage of anger follows a confirmation of the bad news. Anger directed at God, your physician (as bearer of the bad news) or misplaced toward loved ones is an emotional reaction to the bad news. In the bargaining phase, the third stage, the dying person looks for ways out of the difficult situation such as making promises to God in exchange for giving up behaviors that led to the terminal illness (e.g., smoking), if given a second change. Bargaining is made with whoever the dying person perceives as having extra-ordinary abilities, including a spiritualist or a physician. When bargaining fails Depression follows and Acceptance is simply waiting for death to happen, having made all efforts with physical, mental, and emotional exhaustion setting in.

Kubler-Ross' stages demonstrate an active effort to resist death by the dying person. The Middle East has 75 million adults who are illiterate and 13 million of these are females who lack health education. When faced with a health crisis such as a cancer, they rather defer to their Islamic teaching of death's timing as determined by Allah or God (e.g., Roudi-Fahami & Moghadam, 2009; http://www.prb.org/pdf/EmpoweringWomeninMENA.pdf). Also, Islam teaches that in the face of suffering that comes with a disease, God rewards patience (Tayeb, Al-Zamel, Fareed, & Abouellail, 2010). Reports show that breast cancer is a common killer disease in the region where the people are culturally and ethnically diverse yet share a common faith in Islam. (e.g., Kristiansen & Sheikh, 2012).

DEATH AND DYING PRACTICES IN ISRAEL

The Middle East includes Israel, considered a Western country because it joins Western Europe and other groups at UN meetings; participates in European International Football forums; and enters the Eurovision Song contest (e.g., Del Sarto, 2014). Of all the countries in the Middle East, Israel has the highest life expectancy at 82.50 years and has practices akin to Western European countries including healthcare. However, Judaism the dominant religion in Israel is professed by 74.2% of the population and is different from the Islamic faith (Israel Central Bureau of Statistics, 2019; Israel's Independence Day 2019 (PDF) (Report). Israel Central Bureau of Statistics. 6 May 2019).

In Judaism hell does not exist (e.g., Boustan, 2004). The Jewish faith is very influential in the death and dying practices in Israel. Common practices include treating the deceased with respect and providing comfort to the bereaved. In accordance with the Jewish faith of ensuring a proper burial, there is a burial society (also known as the *Chevra Kadis*) comprising of volunteer men and women who ensure that the body is ritually cleansed and shrouded, prior to burial (Jewishfuneralguide.com, n.d.; http://www.jewish-funeral-guide.com /tradition/chevra-kadisha.htm/). Male members of the burial society also help in digging graves if gravediggers are not available. Burial should take place shortly after death, thus allowing viewing of the body before burial becoming difficult especially for far-away relatives. Cremation and embalming are forbidden because the body should be allowed to decompose naturally (Chabad.org,n.d.; https://www .chabad.org/library/article_cdo/aid/510874/jewish/Why-Does -Judaism-Forbid-Cremation.htm).

Funeral service in Israel is brief and takes place at the burial ground and includes reading of psalms, a eulogy, and a closing prayer. The initial mourning period occurs in the first seven days, called *Shiva.* Visitors gather at the home of the mourner, who pays less attention to personal appearance such as bathing, shaving, wearing leather shoes or jewelry. Customarily in Shiva the mourner sits on a low stool or even the floor symbolizing an emotional low brought about by grief. Since the mourner avoids any cooking or household work during this period, guests help with food, household chores, and taking care of little children or running errands. Shloshim is the 30 days after burial and mourning continues in various ways, including forbidding the mourner from marrying. Mourning a parent lasts for 12 months (known as *Shneim asar chodesh*). Although the mourner re-engages in most activities during this period, there are restriction in attending festivities and enjoying loud music. Some deaths are difficult to grieve, because they are not socially sanctioned (e.g., Doka's, 2002 disenfranchised grief). They include physician-assisted suicide and euthanasia, which are forbidden by both Israeli Penal Law and Jewish law (Chabad.org, n.d.;https://www.chabad.org/library/article _cdo/aid/510874/jewish/Why-Does-Judaism-Forbid-Cremation.htm). Judaism and the Islamic religion converges in forbidding cremation, but not in the time line for mourning.

Key Terms

Communication
Judaism
Islamic beliefs

Islamic teachings
Israel
Middle East region
Muslims
Sensitivity
Western practices

SUMMARY

1. Islam is the dominant religion in the Middle East, influencing death and dying beliefs and practices.
2. Islamic teachings run counter to Western medical practices, hence the important of Western-trained physicians to be sensitive in styles of communication.
3. The Islamic teachings may have impact on Western models of bereavement and dying (e.g., Worden's four tasks of mourning and Kubler-Ross's five stages of dying).
4. Non-communicable diseases are the predominant causes of death in the region.
5. Among the Saudis spiritual healing, Islamic beliefs, and traditional healing are options to Western medical care models.

Review Questions

1. How can Islamic teachings influence the health-seeking behaviors of Muslims?
2. Can Westernization influences co-exist with the Islamic religion?
3. Do Islamic beliefs have influences on Worden's Four Tasks of mourning and Kubler-Ross's stages of dying?
4. How might a Western trained physician exercise sensitivity in communicating with a Saudi Muslim patient?
5. Are there differences and similarities between Islam and Judaism in burial and bereavement practices?

Additional Readings

Charles, C. E., & Daroszewski, E. B. (2012). Culturally competent nursing care of the Muslim patient. *Issues Ment Health Nurs., 33:* 61–63.
Sachedina, A. (2005). End-of-life: the Islamic view. *Lancet, 366:* 774–779.

Baddarni, K. (2010). Ethical dilemmas and the dying Muslim patient. *Asian Pac J Cancer Prev, 11:* 107–112

Harford, J. B., & Aljawi, D. M. (2013). The need for more and better palliative care for Muslim patients. *Palliat Support Care, 11:* 1–4.

Chapter 5

DEATH, DYING AND BEREAVEMENT
IN NORTH AMERICA

Chapter Outline

Learning objectives
Life expectancy and the prevalent causes of death
Influence of religion on death and dying beliefs and practices in
    North America
Christian beliefs and practices on death and dying
Indigenous religious beliefs and practices on death and dying
Influence of belief systems on death rituals and practices
Death and dying among minority ethnic groups
African Americans
Hispanics
Native Americans/Indigenous peoples
The Coast Salish or Indigenous people
The Cree nation
Key terms
Summary
Review questions
Additional readings

Learning Objectives

LO1: Understand the levels of development and life expectancy of
      countries in North America
LO2: Understand the predominant causes of death in North America
      as reflected by the countries' levels of development

LO3: Explain death, dying and bereavement practices and beliefs that reflect upon Individualism and Collectivism

LO4: Explain death, dying and bereavement beliefs and practices that reflect upon Individualism

LO5: Describe death, dying and bereavement beliefs and practices that reflect upon accommodation behavior

LO6: Describe traditional religious beliefs and practices in death, dying and bereavement

LO7: Understand Christian religious beliefs and practices in death, dying and bereavement

LIFE EXPECTANCY AND PREVALENT CAUSES OF DEATH

With the exception of Haiti and Belize, countries in North America have life expectancy in the 70 and 80 year age range. Canada is the highest at 81.90 years. The prevailing causes of death in most of the countries are communicable diseases. Figure 5.1 shows life expectancy estimated at birth in various countries in 2017.

Figure 5.1
Life Expectancy of Countries in North American Estimated at Birth, 2017

Country	Life Expectancy (in years)
Canada	81.90
United States	80.00
Costa Rica	78.70
Cuba	78.80
Panama	78.80
Antigua and Barbuda	76.70
Mexico	76.10
Bahamas	72.60
Barbados	75.50

continued

Figure 5.1—*Continued*

Country	Life Expectancy (in years)
Jamaica	73.70
Nicaragua	73.50
Saint Lucia	77.90
Dominica Republic	77.20
El Salvador	74.90
Grenada	74.50
Trinidad and Tobago	73.10
Guatemala	72.60
Honduras	71.20
Belize	68.90
Haiti	64.20

Source: CIA: The World Factbook; https://www.cia.gov/library/publications/the-world-factbook/rankorder/2102rank.html

As noted in earlier chapters, the World Bank (2020) classifies countries that have less than $1,025 Gross National Income per capita as low-income countries, those with between $1,026 and $3,0995 as lower-middle income countries, those with between $3,996 and $12,375 as upper-middle income countries, and those with incomes of more than $12,376 as high-income countries (datahelpdesk.World Bank.org, 2020). Most of the countries fit under the high income and upper-middle income categories. Haiti however fits into a nomenclature of its own (low income category), being the poorest in the Western hemisphere (e.g., World Bank Group, 2020).

The top 10 leading causes of death in both high and upper-middle income economies are presented in Figure 5.3.

Figure 5.2
Map of North America

Source: Istockphoto.com

Figure 5.3
Top 10 Killer Diseases in High and Upper Middle Income Countries

High Income Countries	Upper Middle Income Countries
Ischaemic heart disease	Ischaemic heart disease
Stroke	Stroke
Alzheimer's disease and other dementias	Chronic obstructive pulmonary disease
Trachea, bronchus, lung cancers	Trachea, bronchus, lung cancers
Chronic obstructive pulmonary disease	Alzheimer's disease and other dementias
Lower respiratory infections	Lower respiratory infection
Colon and rectum cancers	Diabetes mellitus
Diabetes mellitus	Road injury
Kidney diseases	Liver cancer
Breast cancer	Stomach cancer

Source: WHO (2018a; https://www.who.int/news-room/fact-sheets/detail/the-top-10-causes-of-death/)

In high or upper-middle income countries non-communicable factors are mostly responsible for death, unlike countries (e.g., Haiti) impacted by the spread of communicable diseases such as diarrheal infections that could kill large swath of people, including children. Communicable diseases such as diarrheal diseases, tuberculosis, and lower respiratory infections are mostly responsible for death in lower-middle income or lower income economies. Already contributing to death are, road injury and preterm birth complications. It is important to have statistics on death causation for a variety of reasons including planning for interventions and determining how to allocate resources in a country's budget.

INFLUENCE OF RELIGION ON DEATH AND DYING
BELIEFS AND PRACTICES IN NORTH AMERICA

Although cultures may differ, religion is very influential in the grieving and death rituals of many people around the world (e.g., Chachkes & Jennings, 1994; Younoszai, 1993).

The USA, Canada, and Mexico make up 85% of the population of North America, with Christianity as the dominant religion in these countries (Pewforum.org, 2011; https://www.pewforum.org/2011/12 /19/global-christianity-regions/). Thus, the Christian religion has the largest following in North America. Within North America, the term "Central America" is also used to describe the location of Guatemala, Belize, Honduras, El Salvador, Nicaragua, Costa Rica, and Panama where the majority of the people are Roman Catholics. While North America (including Central America) has a pervasive Christian influence, there are also Indigenous religious belief and practices that coexist with Christianity in death, dying and bereavement practices. This demonstrates accommodation behavior.

Christian Beliefs and Practices on Death and Dying

Generally, Christian beliefs and practices are guided by afterlife beliefs. After death, mourners, including family members and friends, observe a "wake" when personal experiences about the departed person are shared. On the third day, special prayers are offered for the deceased, depicting the resurrection of Christ from the grave. A funeral mass for the deceased is held in church or after the body is buried, a memorial service is conducted (e.g., Marshall & Sutherland, 2008). Christians believe in heaven and hell, with God as the judge of one's final location. People who lived a godly life and accepted Christ as Savior prior to death would go to heaven, a place sometimes referred to as paradise. Hell is devoid of God's love and is reserved for ungodly people who do not accept Christ as Savior prior to death. Catholics believe in both heaven and hell, but also in Purgatory; a place where people with "forgivable" sins go to be purged of their sins before being admitted into heaven (BBC.com, 2009; https://www.bbc.co.uk /religion/religions/christianity/ritesrituals/funerals.shtml/). Last Rites are given by a priest to a dying person as opportunity to reconcile with God and ask for forgiveness. For a Christian, Funeral depicts a triumphant entry into heaven; with hymns song and prayers and exhortations said from the Bible, as in 1 Corinthians 15:55-57 King James Version (KJV):

> [55] *O death, where is thy sting? O grave, where is thy victory?*
> [56] *The sting of death is sin; and the strength of sin is the law.*
> [57] *But thanks be to God, which giveth us the victory through our Lord Jesus Christ.*

During Committal service at the cemetery a short prayer is also said by the priest, with the tradition of throwing dust/mud unto the coffin signifying ashes to ashes, dust to dust (BBC.com, 2019).

Indigenous Religious Beliefs and Practices on Death and Dying

Although Christianity is North America's dominant religion, many countries in the region also have Afro-Caribbean or Indigenous religious practices. For example, a Pewforun.org (2014; https://www.pew forum.org/2014/11/13/religion-in-latin-america/) survey reports that in the region many people believe in "evil eye"—a belief, associated with indigenous religions that certain people can put a spell on others that can cause them harm or lead to death.

Figure 5.4
Percentage of Christians (Catholic and Protestant) who believe in "evil eye"

Country	Percentage of Catholics who believe in evil eye	Percentage of Protestants who believe in evil eye
Panama	69	49
Dominican Republic	58	47
Honduras	55	55
Nicaragua	46	51
El Salvador	53	40
Costa Rica	38	44

continued

Figure 5.4—*Continued*

Country	Percentage of Catholics who believe in evil eye	Percentage of Protestants who believe in evil eye
Mexico	45	18
Puerto Rico	45	28
Guatemala	41	28

Source: Pewforun.org (2014; https://www.pewforum.org/2014/11/13/religion-in-latin-america/

On average, there are more professed Catholics than Protestants who believe in evil eye, and the percentage of believers is over 50% in Panama, Dominican Republic, Honduras and El Salvador. Also, there is an equally high percentage of Protestants who believe in evil eye in these countries (including Nicaragua). In addition to evil eye the Pew Research Center's (2014) survey identifies seven other Indigenous religious beliefs, which include reincarnation, witchcraft or sorcery, communicating with spirits, and offering food drinks or flowers to spirits. Other types include participating in spiritual cleansing ceremonies, consulting spiritual healers, and experiencing black magic. Of the people surveyed in the different countries, not less than 30% claimed to have indulged in at least three (including evil eye) of the 8 Indigenous religious practices. In Panama, the percentage of people who participated in these practices was 58%, and in Mexico and Honduras it was 44% and 42%, respectively. Figure 5.5 provides, as an example, some religious beliefs and practices in North America.

Based on the triarchical environmental dimensions discussed in earlier chapters, most countries in North America (particularly in Central America) approach death and dying based on a combination of Western and indigenous religious beliefs, a phenomenon known as accommodation behavior. Most people in the region embrace Christianity but without putting aside their Indigenous religion, which is a representation of their culture and their personhood. Historically, colonialists from Britain, France and Spain; and Christian missionaries had encounters with African slaves in the 17th and 19th centuries,

Figure 5.5
Some Indigenous Religions of North America

Indigenous Religion	Beliefs on death and dying	Country where practiced
Santería (worship of saints; blending Indigenous religion with Roman Catholicism)	Divination on death causation; healing from evil spirits (e.g., Du Toit, 2001; De La Torre, 2004; Rosario & De La Rosa, 2014)	Cuba, Puerto Rico, Dominican Republic, Panama, USA
Vodou (or Voodoo)	Death resulting from ignoring a Loa—an Intermediary between humans and Supreme God (e.g., Simpson, 1980). Death is transition from one life to another.	Haiti; Dominican Republic, Cuba, Bahamas, USA
Espiritismo	Good and evil spirits affect health and other aspects of life	Puerto Rico, Cuba (e.g., Anderson, 2015)

Source: Author's creation.

and the effects have led to a combination of religious practices experienced in the region (e.g., Beasley, 2009).

In Barbados, where majority of the people are of African descent, many believe in spirits yet are Christians as a result of colonialism. People do not visit the grave of a deceased loved one because they believe that "duppies" or "jupies" (local names for spirits) inhabit the cemeteries. According to researcher Camille Huggins and her colleague, Glenda HInkson (2019) duppies are believed to come out at night and people claim to have seen them. The practice of a "wake" or gathering at the home of the deceased's family does not occur until after the funeral because of a strong belief in the presence of duppies associated with the presence of dead people.

In Haiti, a former French colony, the majority (95%) of the people also are of African descent, with an estimated 83% in 2003 professing Christianity (CIA, World Factbook, https://www.cia.gov/library/publications/the-world-factbook/geos/ha.html; n.d.). Yet, the practice of Vodou (a mixture of African and Catholic practices) is common among Haitians, in death and dying rituals (e.g., Rey & Stepick, 2013). Among Vodou practitioners, there is a belief that God is too busy attending to many things of the world, therefore the need for lesser gods or spirits to act as an intermediary (some researcher believe it's synonymous to Saints in the Catholic tradition). During funerals, a vodou priest is hired to intercede with the Intermediary god or Loa; and a lot of drumming, singing, and dancing goes on. As a sign of respect, funeral participants offer the vodou priest money, alcohol, and cigars. The vodou priest in turn gives prophecy, and cleanses or blesses the people (e.g., Rey & Stepick, 2013).

The tradition of the *nine-night* is based on the belief that the deceased's soul hovers around and does not depart to its final resting place until the 9th day. Ahead of the 9th day, each day is spent in prayers and in preparation for the home-going celebration of the deceased (e.g., Simpson, 1980). Haitians believe that for guidance and protection, the spirit of ancestors need to be worshipped; failing which the dead can return to cause havoc on the living resulting in mental illnesses, accidents, or untimely deaths. Therefore, funerals involve not just Christian practices, but also Vodou rituals due to traditional beliefs (e.g., Rey & Spetick, 2013).

Espiritismo (Portuguese and Spanish for spiritism), found in Puerto Rico and Cuba, among other places is a variant of an indigenous religion that combines Indigenous religious practices with Christianity. Practitioners of espiritismo believe in the existence of a Supreme God, but also in good and evil spirits being able to influence health outcomes and other aspects of a person's well-being. The practice involves Ancestor worship and communing with dead loved ones (e.g., Anderson, 2015).

INFLUENCE OF BELIEF SYSTEMS ON DEATH RITUALS AND PRACTICES

Researchers Sandra Lobar and colleagues (2006) conducted a focus group study of participants from different cultures and reported a common theme. The type of rituals and ceremonies that need to be performed is influenced by beliefs in what becomes of the deceased person's soul in the afterlife. The stronger the belief, the more dedicated family members would be in ensuring that the appropriate rituals and ceremonies are performed, and in accordance with the dictates of their religion and/or culture. In this regard, bereaved loved ones might find it difficult to separate cultural practices from religious beliefs of contrary views. Therefore, based on cultural beliefs most African descendants in Central America combine Christianity with Indigenous religious practices in death and dying practices (e.g., Spector, 2002).

USA AND CANADA: DEATH, DYING AND BEREAVEMENT PRACTICES

Both the USA and Canada have a predominantly White population. In 2019 Whites make up 76.5 % of the US (US Census Bureau; https://www.census.gov/quickfacts/fact/table/US/RHI125218/), whereas in 2016 Canadians of European origin make up 72.9% of the population of Canada (Statistics Canada, Census Profile 2016 Census; https://www12.statcan.gc.ca/census-recensement/2016/dp-pd/prof/details/page.cfm?Lang=E&Geo1=PR&Code1=01&Geo2=PR&Code2=01&Data=Count&SearchText=canada&SearchType=Begins&SearchPR=01&B1=All&TABID=1/). Thus, in both countries the Western culture of independence or individualism is pervasive and that helps to guide death rituals and practices, both before and after a loss. A good example of individualism is the practice involved in end-of-life decision making. In the USA physician-assisted suicide is legal in 8 states and in Washington DC and also in Canada. Physician-assisted suicide is the decision that an individual voluntarily makes to end his or her life with the assistance of a physician who prescribes a lethal dose of medication to be administered by the dying person (American Medical Association (n.d.); https://www.ama-assn.org/delivering-care/ethics/physician-assisted-suicide). In the USA, 4,249 prescriptions for physician-assisted suicide (PAS) were issued between 1998–2017. Of the 66.3% patients who used the drugs to end their lives, 94.2% were White (euthanasia.procon.org, 2019; https://euthanasia.procon.org/state-by-state-physician-assisted-suicide-statistics/). Reasons mostly provided for seeking physician-assisted suicide included loss of enjoyment with life, loss of independence, and loss of dignity. All these reasons reflect the values of individualism.

Researcher Herbert Northcott and colleague Donna Wilson (2016) note that in both the USA and Canada, post-death rituals include a eulogy given on the deceased and opportunity to offer support through donations to charitable or research organizations. Expressions of sympathy are made through sympathy cards, verbal expressions, flowers, or attendance at funeral service. Forms of final act on the dead body include below ground burial, mausoleum burial or cremation. Generally, the choice of final act on the dead body is in tune with the deceased person's wishes, which could be novel (e.g., donation to science or burial under the water). After burial, workplace bereavement policies require that the survivor resumes full-blown work shortly after (Eyetsemitan, 1998). Oftentimes memorials for the deceased are linked to landscape, e.g., cemeteries, roadside, battlegrounds, or gardens and rivers for scattered cremains (Baptist, 2010). The landscape is tangible and it symbolizes the memory of the deceased.

Grief theories recommend practices that would help the bereaved person to get back to normalcy. As described in an earlier chapter, William Worden (2008) recommends four tasks that bereaved persons need to accomplish to get back to normal life: 1) accept the reality of the loss; 2) work through the pain of the loss; 3) adjust to the deficits created by the loss; and 4) find a lasting connection to the deceased while moving on with life, including forming new relationships. Thus, to get back to normalcy bereaved persons should actively (and not passively) confront their grief.

DEATH AND DYING AMONG MINORITY ETHNIC GROUPS

The USA and Canada have minority ethnic groups that do not fit into the individualistic mold of the dominant White culture of individualism that is reflective in bereavement models.

African Americans

Researchers Anna Laurie and Robert Neimeyer (2008) report that when compared to Caucasians, African Americans hardly speak to others about their loss including professional grief counselors and are more likely to have complicated grief symptoms. Also, African Americans are more likely to experience death from homicide, experience greater loss of extended family members, and maintain continuing attachment with deceased loved ones in a spiritual way (e.g., Kochanek, Murphy, Anderson, & Scott, 2004; Laurie & Neimeyer, 2008). They also have a shorter life expectancy and are more likely to experience the premature death of parents, siblings and relatives (Rosenblatt & Wallace, 2005). In 2014, the average life expectancy of African Americans was 75.2 years, compared to Whites at 78.8 years (CDC, 2016; https://www.cdc.gov/nchs/products/databriefs/db244.htm/).

Premature death, poverty, and racism place African Americans in a unique situation to handle death and dying differently. And in a more collectivistic way (e.g., Rosenblatt & Wallace, 2005). In the African American community, because of the range of people who can pass as "loved ones," in bereavement the black experience becomes complex and is likely to influence African Americans' worldview of sorrow and suffering (e.g., Gillies & Neimeyer, 2006; Neimeyer, 2001). According to Robert Weiss (1988), bereavement is more intense in a loss that involves "primary relationships" (e.g., parent, spouse, child) than in "secondary relationships" (e.g., extended family members, acquaintances). However, with Blacks, the loss of a fictive kin (secondary relationship) could also be as intense as a blood relative (e.g., Hines, 1991). Blacks experience a higher rate of complicated grief (unresolved grief) when compared to Caucasians (Goldsmith et al, 2008). However, participation in church activities does provide a supportive network and spiritual coping. In coping with a loss African Americans are more likely to approach their pastors than professionals (Taylor, Chatters, & Jackson, 2007). There are studies that point to a positive relationship between religious beliefs and psychological well-being (e.g., Frazier, Mintz, & Mobley, 2005).

African Americans also turn to social support from family, friends, and fictive kin who are not blood relatives (akin to Africans where the word "brother," "sister," "dad," or "mom" is used beyond blood relatives) (e.g., Sudarkasa, 1997; Rosenblatt & Wallace, 2005). Family members are obligated to attend funerals, including children (e.g., Schoulte, 2011); and open caskets at a wake and/or church service are encouraged during viewing, allowing the bereaved to be comforted by family and friends through hugging, touching, kissing, and spiritual support (e.g., prayers). Meals are provided by friends and family members during the wake and after the funerals. Funerals are arranged with a view to fostering community support and engagement (e.g.,

Moore, 2003). The involvement of family and community in African American funerals has its origins in West African cultures, where burials are elaborate social events that can go on for several days. When compared to White American funerals, African American funerals are often hours longer (e.g., Atkins, 2012).

African Americans maintain ties to deceased loved ones by marking the occasion of their birth or death (e.g., Winston, 2003) and in conversations (e.g., Sullivan, 1995). They believe death is a continuation of life in another realm. Cremation is less preferred to earth burial because of religious and cultural beliefs that the soul will be prevented from getting into heaven (e.g., Lobar, Youngblut & Brooten, 2006). Brooks, Haskins, and Kehe (2004) however note that the term *African American* also applies to immigrants from West Africa, Central America, and South America who believe in and practice Ancestor worship. Therefore, in death, dying and bereavement issues, the practices of the African American community may not be uniform.

Hispanics

The Hispanic community has burial rituals that are greatly influenced by Catholicism. They include an open casket service and reciting of the rosary (e.g., Clements et al., 2003). Also, group prayers are said for the deceased 1–2 evenings before the funeral service and a pastor leads the prayer for guidance of the soul of the deceased (e.g., Diaz-Cabello, 2004). The wake or "velorios" provides an occasion for friends and family members to gather and reflect on their relationships with the deceased and pay their condolences (e.g., Parry & Ryan, 1995). During the initial period of bereavement, immediate family members deny themselves of any pleasures of life (e.g., watching television or attending social events), pray the rosary each day for 9 days (or "novenas"); and in the first anniversary marking the death, they light candles and hold mass in celebration (e.g., Clements et al., 2003; Munet-Vilaro, 1998).

Native Americans/Indigenous Peoples

The Native American community is not homogenous, yet in death and dying experiences a common theme can be found. Native Americans for the most part believe that death is part of the natural cycle of life which is controlled by God the Creator or Great Spirit (e.g.,

Figure 5.6
A Comparison of Native Americans and European
Americans in Death and Dying Beliefs and Practices

Traditional Native American Beliefs and Practices	European American (White) Beliefs and Practices
Death and life are circular	Death and life are linear; emphasis is on self or individual
Death is unknown and subject to supernatural power and therefore should be accepted	Scientific evidence helps in explaining death
Spiritual world exists in the afterlife	Belief in the afterlife varies, but generally there is a belief in heaven (and hell) based on Christian views
Treatment and care decision are family based	Treatment and care decision are individual or appointed proxy based
Communication is implied through silence	Communication is made explicitly
Contract is by oral tradition	Contract is signed documentation

Source: Colclough, Y (2016). Native American Death Taboo: Implications for healthcare providers. *American Journal of Hospice and Palliative Medicine;* 1–8.

Utter, 2002; Turner-Weeden, 1995). In Figure 5.6 a comparison between Native Americans and European Americans illustrates differences in approach to death, dying and bereavement.

While Figure 5.6 appears dichotomous, it is important to note that Native Americans and European Americans may not strictly conform to the practices ascribed to them, due to a dominant Christian influence and acculturation factors resulting from interracial marriages.

The Coast Salish or Indigenous People

The Coast Salish or Indigenous people (Salish-speaking Native Indians located in the northwest USA and west coast of Canada) through acculturation, combine traditional religion with Catholicism and other European beliefs (e.g., Joseph, 1995). However, the level of acculturation influences differ from one person to another. For example, following the death of their father, Joseph (1995) noted the case of two sisters who respectively followed Christian and Indigenous religious routes in dealing with their losses. While one sister relied on the Church and prayer in dealing with her grief, the other used Indigenous religious methods such as water, cedar, devil's club (a shrub) for purification (due to exposure to the corpse). She also sent selected items to the deceased by burning; and approached a medicine man for ministration. Although both sisters sought different approaches in coping with their grief, their father's funeral was a combination of Christian and Indigenous religious practices. On the third day after the death, the wake was held and a funeral followed on the fourth day at the church and graveside; combining Catholic and Indigenous traditions, including burning of clothes and other items they thought the deceased would need in the spirit world.

The Cree Nation

Researcher Mary Hampton and colleagues (2010) interviewed elders from the Cree nation, another Indigenous people (Canada's most populous indigenous group) found in several communities in Canada and the USA. The researchers report that the Cree tribe view death as a transition, and much is expected of family and community members in providing support at the point of dying. People are encouraged not to cry as this could hinder the dying person's transition to the other world. After death there are feasts, prayers, chants, and songs to mark an on-going relationship between the living and the dead (e.g., Hampton et al., 2010). The USA and Canada also have immigrant populations from different parts of the world (e.g., Indians, Chinese, Middle Easterners), espousing other religious beliefs about death, dying and bereavement. Most immigrant groups are likely to adhere to cultural practices of their native land or combine their practices with Christianity.

Key Terms

Afterlife beliefs
Catholicism
Central America
Christianity
Colonialism

Evil eye
Heritage
Indigenous religion
Minority ethnic groups
North America

SUMMARY

1. The USA, Canada, and Mexico make up 85% of the population of North America and Christianity is the dominant religion in each of these countries.
2. The members of minority ethnic groups practice other religions in addition to Christianity, resulting in a dual belief system known as accommodation behavior. For example, in many North American countries the people profess Christianity yet believe in "evil eye," a belief system of indigenous religions.
3. Whites or people of European ancestry are the dominant groups in the USA and Canada, and the cultures of both countries are largely individualistic, as portrayed in end-of-life decisions. For example, in the US, between 1998-2017, 4,249 prescriptions for Physician Assisted Suicide (PAS) were issued and of the 66.3% patients who used the drugs to end their lives, 94.2% were Whites. On the contrary, minority ethnic group members (e.g., African Americans) are largely collectivistic, in their beliefs and practices involving death, dying and bereavement.

Review Questions

1. Do people who opt for physician-assisted suicide lack social support? Discuss
2. Can social support structures help in preventing decisions on physician-assisted suicide?
3. Do you believe in "evil eye?" Why or why not?
4. What are the advantages or disadvantages in having a dual belief in Christianity and Indigenous religion?
5. What Indigenous religious practices are similar or dissimilar to Christian practices in death, dying and bereavement?

Additional Readings

Samuel, L. R. (2013). *Death, American style: A cultural history of dying in America.* Lanham, MD: Rowman & Littlefield.

Chapter 6

DEATH, DYING AND BEREAVEMENT
IN SOUTH AMERICA

Chapter Outline

Learning objectives
Countries of South America
Life expectancy and prevalent causes of death
Religion in South America
Religion, culture and grief models
Deceased-focused approach to mourning: a proposed model
Key terms
Summary
Review questions
Additional readings

Learning Objectives

LO1: Understand the different levels of development of countries in South America

LO2: Describe the predominant causes of death in South America

LO3: Explain death, dying and bereavement beliefs and practices that reflect on Collectivism

LO4: Explain death, dying and bereavement beliefs and practices that reflect on Individualism

LO5: Describe death, dying and bereavement practices that reflect on Accommodation behavior

LO6: Explain Continuing Bond between the living and the dead

LO7: Understand the Deceased-focused model of bereavement

COUNTRIES OF SOUTH AMERICA

The countries of South America include:

Argentina
Bolivia
Brazil
Chile
Colombia
Ecuador
Guyana
Paraguay
Peru
Suriname
Uruguay
Venezuela

Figure 6.1
Map of Countries of South America

Source: Istockphoto.com

LIFE EXPECTANCY AND PREVALENT CAUSES OF DEATH

Brazil is the largest and most populous country in the region, whereas Suriname, the only country where Dutch is the official language, is the smallest. The dominant languages spoken across the region are Portuguese and Spanish. As shown in Figure 6.2 Bolivia and Guyana are the only countries with life expectancy below 70 years of age, whereas the others are in the 70-year age range.

As previously stated in other chapters, in the World Bank (2020) classification countries with less than $1,025 Gross National Income per capita are low-income countries, those with between $1,026 and $30,995 are lower-middle income countries, those with between

Figure 6.2
Life Expectancy of Countries in South American Estimated at Birth, 2017

Country	Life Expectancy (in years)
Chile	78.90
Uruguay	77.40
Argentina	77.30
Brazil	74.00
Colombia	75.90
Peru	74.00
Venezuela	76.00
Ecuador	77.00
Paraguay	77.40
Suriname	72.50
Bolivia	69.50
Guyana	68.60

Source: The World Factbook; https://www.cia.gov/library/publications/the-world -factbook/rankorder/2102rank.html

$3,996 and $12,375 are upper middle-income countries, and those with incomes of more than $12,376 are high-income countries (data-helpdesk.WorldBank.org, 2020).

Both Chile and Uruguay are high-income countries. The rest are either lower middle-income or upper middle-income countries. Majority of the countries fit under the upper middle-income nations which has the top 10 killer diseases/factors as (WHO, 2018):

- Ischaemic heart disease
- Stroke
- Chronic obstructive pulmonary disease
- Trachea, bronchus, lung cancers
- Lower respiratory infection
- Alzheimer's disease and other dementias
- Diabetes mellitus
- Road injury
- Liver cancer
- Stomach cancer

Most of the killer factors are non-communicable, but in lower middle-income countries including Bolivia and Guyana communicable diseases such as diarrheal diseases, tuberculosis, and lower respiratory infections are more prevalent factors for the cause of death (WHO, 2018).

RELIGIONS IN SOUTH AMERICA

As discussed in previous chapters, religion is an influential factor in death, dying and bereavement beliefs and practices. In most countries of South America Christianity is the dominant religion, with the majority of people professing Catholicism, except in Guyana where Catholics are the minority (7%) and Protestants (55%) the majority. In Suriname, however, Christians make up less than half of the population (48.4%), the only country in the region with less than 50% Christian population (Britannica.com, n.d.; Suriname https://www.britannica.com/place/Suriname/People). Figure 6.3 shows the percentage distribution of Christians in the various countries.

Figure 6.3
Christianity in Countries of South America

Country	Catholic (in percentage)	Protestant (in percentage)	Total (in percentage)
Paraguay	89	7	96
Colombia	79	13	92
Ecuador	79	13	92
Bolivia	77	16	93
Peru	76	17	93
Venezuela	73	17	90
Argentina	71	15	86
Chile	64	17	81
Brazil	61	26	87
Uruguay	42	15	57
Suriname	21.6	26.8	48.4
Guyana	7	55	62

Sources: Pew Research 2014; https://www.pewforum.org/2014/11/13/religion-in-latin -america/) Bureau of Statistics, Guyana 2016; *Guyana 2012 census compendium 2.* https://www.google.com/search?q=Guyana+2012+census+compendium+2.&oq=Guy ana+2012+census+compendium+2.&aqs=chrome..69i57j33l4.1413j0j7&sourceid=chro me&ie=UTF-8;) Britannica.com; Suriname https://www.britannica.com/place /Suriname/People).

As discussed in previous chapters, Christians believe in heaven and hell in the afterlife. Heaven is a place believers go to having lived an acceptable life based on the precepts set out for believers and for accepting Christ as savior. Hell, as the opposite, is a place of utter condemnation and devoid of God's love and forgiveness and is reserved for those who before death lived ungodly lives and failed to accept Christ as savior. Catholics believe in Purgatory as a place where 'forgivable" sins are eliminated, before entry into heaven.

The nations of South America are racially and ethnically heterogenous making the region one of the most diverse in the world. There are people of European, European-Amerindian or Mestizo (mixed Spanish), Amerindians, African, and Mullato (mixed White and Black) (e.g.,Brittanica.com, n.d.; Latin America; https://www.brittannica.com/topic/race-human/Latin-America). Due to the racial ethnic diversity, people blend other religions with Christianity, or practice their indigenous religions separately. For example, in Brazil, Afro-Brazilian religions, including *Candomble* and *Umbanda,* are brought by Black slaves from Africa. Practitioners of these religions believe in spirits and they summon their gods with chants and dances and worship them with food, candles, and flowers left at public places. There are two million followers of *Candomble* which is also practiced in Argentina, Uruguay, Paraguay and Venezuela. *Umbanda,* another Afro-Brazilian religion, blends African tradition (e.g., belief in spirit, use of intermediary mediums to contact spirit of dead people and reincarnation) with Roman Catholicism. This religion also has following in Argentina and Uruguay (e.g., Phillips 2015). Yet, many who practice Afro-Brazilian religions also profess Christianity (accommodation behavior).

Researcher Regina Bousso and colleagues (2011) conducted an interview with 17 Brazilian families of different religious backgrounds (e.g., Catholic, Protestant, Umbanda, Buddhism and Spiritism) who had experienced the loss of a loved one. One family member said neither Catholicism nor Protestantism could provide an answer for the loss of their loved one, but Spiritism did. In their grief resolution, seeking an explanation for a loss was important; and this may not be provided by Christian beliefs or Western autopsy reports. In Regina Bousso and colleagues' (2011) study, the explanation provided by the non-Western/indigenous dimension of the triarchical environment through Spiritism was more important in grief resolution.

In Brazil where 87% of the population profess Christianity, almost half of the population have visited an Umbanda worship center at least once, especially during a time of personal crisis (e.g., Chestnut, 2003). Anthropologist Guilherme Velho (2003) puts it this way:

> The vast majority of Brazilian society is made up Roman Catholics. However, there are endless and frequent examples of Catholics attending spiritist centers and umbanda and candomblé rituals.

When they do not do this in person, they use friends and relatives as
intermediaries. Illness, employment and love are some of the issues
which may lead traditional Catholics and Protestants, Jews, Atheists,
Agnostics etc., to seek help, advice and solutions with spirits of light,
pretos velhos, Ogum, Xangô, and, why not, exus and pombas-giras.
(Velho, 2003, p. 25)

RELIGION, CULTURE AND GRIEF MODELS

As described in earlier chapters, William Worden's (2008) grief
model suggests that a bereaved person needs to complete four tasks
following a loss: 1) acknowledge the loss; 2) feel the pain of the loss;
3) replace the role (s) of the deceased; and 4) memorialize the
deceased while moving on with life. However, for many Brazilians
who practice indigenous religions (or in combination with Christianity), memorializing the deceased and moving on with their lives,
would first require a satisfactory answer for their loss beyond what
Western medical autopsy reports or Christian beliefs could provide.
Therefore, the answer to the "why the loss" question is complex
which requires resolution before Worden's last stage is commenced. It
is suggested that the resolution of the "why the loss" question should
precede Worden's fourth stage of memorializing the deceased and
moving on with life.

Dennis Klass and colleagues' (1996) model of Continuing Bond
with the deceased contrasts with Worden's (2008) fourth stage of
memorializing the deceased and moving on with life. In continuing
bond an active, ongoing relationship with the deceased is described
contrary to a detachment from the deceased (after memorialization).
It also negates the Freudian psycho-analytical approach of breaking
ties with the past to becoming free (e.g., Freud, 1952). However, to
maintain continuing bond with the deceased is an individual's choice
(e.g., Field, 2008; Stroebe & Schut, 2005). Continuing bond could be
maintained either explicitly (e.g., writing letters) or implicitly (e.g.,
mental recalls of the past). In recalling the past, for example, the
bereaved person may remember how her deceased grandmother used
to prepare her favorite pie or what she would have said or done in a
given situation in the future (e.g., Heckhausen & Schultz, 1995).
Memorials as suggested by Worden (2008), could also double as forms
of continuing bonds. In Figure 6.4, a distinction is made between

Figure 6.4
Examples of Memorial and Continuing Bond

Memorial	**Continuing Bond**
Statue	Letter writing
Park	Dreams
Building	Naming a child after a deceased Parent
Church service	Talking to the deceased
Plaque	Tatoo
Tatoo	Webpage
Scholarship	Poetry
Webpage	Wearing a deceased's ashes in a locket
Monument	Visit to sites where the deceased was buried
Gift	Feeling the presence of the deceased

Source: Author's creation.

memorials and continuing bonds which in certain instances could overlap, e.g., a tatoo or a webpage.

Researcher Terrah Foster and colleagues (2012) conducted a qualitative study in Ecuador of 49 participants and explored how bereaved persons maintain continuing bond with deceased loved ones. They identified two types of continuing bond: 1) purposeful bond and 2) non-purposeful bond. Purposeful bond identified by 98% of the participants included keeping personal belongings/photographs, talking/praying to the deceased, enjoying activities the deceased participated in while alive, and visiting the cemetery. Non-purposeful bond which was identified by 61% of participants included dreams about and visits from the deceased (in the form of feeling the presence of the deceased). A majority (71%) of the participants find comfort in continuing bond, but 55% say they find it discomfiting. Foster and colleagues (2012) note that the nature of continuing bond they found among Ecuadorians was pretty consistent across cultures (e.g., keeping photographs or belongings of the deceased, talking to the deceased, having dreams about the deceased, or feeling the presence of the deceased). What might differ, however, is the percentage of those comforted or discomforted in maintaining such bonds, which might be influenced by religious beliefs or cultural practices. For example, among the Chinese, Cecilia Chan and colleagues (2005) note that Taoist priests advise bereaved persons to expect the deceased's spirit to visit them from time to time.

Psychologically, continuing bond could elicit pain, hurt or guilt feelings, especially in the death of a young child or suicide. The effect of guilt may cut both ways, however. On the one hand, it may cause the bereaved to be uneasy with continuing bond especially with self-blame, whereas on the other it makes the bereaved want to demonstrate affection with the deceased. Foster and others (2012) note that some participants report discomfort maintaining continuing bond when the death is untimely deaths, such as when the loved one(s) passed away suddenly from a drug overdose or accident.

As earlier mentioned, Suriname is the smallest country in South America where Dutch is the official language spoken. According to the World Bank (2018b) (https://data.worldbank.org/indicator/SP .POP.TOTL?locations=SR), Suriname has a population of less than 1million people (575,911) and is made up of diverse ethnicities, e.g., East Indians, Javanese, Amerindians, Chinese, Dutch, Portuguese, Jews, and Africans (from slave trade) who make up about 37% of the population. The population of Afro-Surinamese include the Creoles (mixed descendants of slaves and Europeans of mostly Dutch) and the Moroons (the descendants of escaped slaves) (Britannica.com, n.d.; https://www.britannica.com/place/Suriname/People). Among Afro-Surinamese, the worlds of the living and the dead are intertwined. While funeral ceremonies are conducted to cut off ties with the deceased, they are also to affirm connections with the spirit of the deceased in the afterlife. Attention is first given to the deceased before the bereaved, by ensuring that the burial is done properly. There is a strong belief that the spirit of the deceased is powerful and able to influence the living, either positively or negatively (e.g., van der Pijl, 2010).

The Afro-Surinamese believe that the spirit of the deceased hovers around for a while before departing to the afterlife. To expedite this departure and cut ties with the deceased's spirit, mirrors, paintings, and pictures are turned around or covered so that the deceased does not see itself and refuse to depart. According to Yvon van der Pijl (2016), among the Creoles widows and widowers place items such as underwear or a handkerchief that has their smell in the deceased's coffin as a decoy to prevent the spirit of the deceased from visiting them. Deceased persons are made to feel that their spouses are still with them. While this appears as breaking ties with the deceased, it also means that the deceased is being made to feel pleased with receiving a "proper" burial.

In Western burials, the deceased person's preference is taken into consideration in funeral arrangements. Among Afro-Surinamese, however, there are standard rituals that need to be followed, according to norms and traditions, in order to ensure a "proper" burial for the deceased. For example, a deceased person's request for cremation may be unusual if it goes against the collective norms and traditions of a proper burial. Yet, a deceased person is believed to be unhappy if his or her wishes are not carried out, by visiting the living with calamities. However, the living can appease the dead through traditional rituals as a recourse.

The Christian religion that many Afro-Surinamese profess, disapproves of traditional religious practices in burial. Family members who subscribe to Christian teachings only and those who believe in traditional religious practices only, may be pitted against each other in burial arrangements for a deceased loved one. However, in Afro-Surinamese burial practices certain symbolic actions satisfy both Christian and Traditional religious worldviews, for different reasons. For example, researcher van der Pijl (2016) reports that prior to the wake (referred to as *dede oso*), a table is set with a white tablecloth, a glass of water and a lit white candle. In the Christian world view the water symbolizes purification and the lit candle hope and resurrection in Christ, whereas in the traditional religion worldview these items connect the living with the dead. Also, whereas the color white represents purity and affinity with Christ, it is the dress code during the period of intense mourning to strengthen a connection with ancestors in traditional religion. After the funeral, another mourning event occurs on the 40th day. Those with Christian views interpret the gathering on the 40th day as coinciding with the death and ascension of Christ. But traditional religion worshippers believe that on the 40th day the spirit of the deceased leaves this earth. Such symbolisms are likely to harmonize Christian and traditional belief systems, thus reducing cognitive dissonance in bereaved persons who subscribe to both belief systems.

Also, due to expediency, the developed/Western triarchical environment may be influential in embracing modernity and technology and allowing for some traditional burial rituals to be circumvented or be replaced. For example, in urban settings, the procession to the cemetery by manually carrying the coffin is being replaced using a hearse, a car or a hired van, instead. Also, shortening the mourning period (e.g., van der Pijl, 2016) may be in conformity with modern workplace bereavement policies or the desire to return to work to earn a living.

DECEASED-FOCUSED APPROACH TO MOURNING: A PROPOSED MODEL

It is being proposed in this model that keeping the deceased "happy" in turn brings about healing to the bereaved. For believers of traditional religion, healing from a loss is accentuated when the deceased person is given a "proper" burial in accordance with tradition and custom. Bereavement theorists recommend that to make a recovery from a loss, bereaved persons should take actions to fill the deficits created by their departed loved ones. As previously stated, William Worden (2008) suggests that the survivor has to accomplish four tasks to get back to normalcy: 1) accept the loss, 2) feel the pain of the loss, 3) adjust to the changes brought about by the loss, and 4) look for ways to memorialize the deceased and move on with life. However, to the practitioner of traditional religion, moving on with life and making a full recovery requires that a proper burial has been accorded the deceased (or, if not, that the deceased be appeased). The deceased's happiness or unhappiness is believed to impact on the living either positively or negatively. Thus, to ensure that the bereaved is healed is also to ensure that the deceased is pleased.

In both Worden's (2008) four tasks of mourning and Stroebe and Schut's (1999) dual process model of grieving, the practical reality of bereaved persons having to adjust to their loss is emphasized. While Worden's (2008) suggests a sequential step-wise process, Margaret Stroebe and Schut's (1999) model suggests that the bereaved person oscillates between Worden's first two steps (*acknowledge the loss and feel the pain*) and the latter two steps (*adjust to the loss and move on*). In both theories, the bereaved person is the focus of attention. However, for traditional religion believers the deceased is instead the focus of attention by ensuring that the dead person is pleased. Dennis Klass and colleagues (1996) in continuing bond suggests that while making practical adjustments for the deceased's absence, the bereaved also wants to make the deceased a part of their lives. For example, bereaved persons write letters to the deceased, talk to the deceased, visit the place where the deceased is interred, or feel the presence of the deceased. Again, the focus of attention is on the bereaved.

The proposed *deceased-focused approach* calls for a different approach. In other words, the bereaved person intentionally does what is pleasing to the deceased if she or he were alive, because the bereaved is aware of the proclivities of the deceased. Ancestor worshippers believe that the deceased is aware of goings-on in the world of the living and has supernatural abilities to help or hurt the bereaved in the afterlife. As mentioned earlier, during burials the bereaved include favorite items in the coffin of the deceased (and among the creoles underwear and handkerchief of the deceased's spouse), believing that such items would be pleasing to the deceased (e.g., Yvon van der Pijl, 2016). With the *deceased-focused approach,* the attempts at pleasing the deceased go beyond burials, however.

Statements have been made by bereaved persons (including non-religious individuals), alluding to attempts at pleasing the deceased after burials. Such statements include:

a. *My spouse would want me to remarry and be happy.*
b. *This funeral is a celebration of Nicole's life because she wouldn't want us to be sad.*
c. *Even though times are hard, I'm sure my father would want us to keep the farm in the family.*

These statements illustrate a bereaved person's willingness to be an extension of the wants or desires of the deceased and to do things that would be pleasing to the deceased. Overcoming grief is not only about the bereaved person having to adjust to his or her own loss. The *deceased* person has experienced a loss, also, and would require help with adjusting to their own loss. By focusing on the deceased, this would help in bringing about satisfaction and healing to the bereaved.

The bereaved, however, should be able to demonstrate the ability to understand the feelings and perspectives of others, as the proposed deceased-focused approach to bereavement is predicated on Robert Selman's perspective-taking theory (1980).

The untimely death of George Floyd on May 25, 2020 caused by police brutality brought about nationwide grief and protests. George Floyd left behind a 6-year-old daughter, Gianna, and his roles in her life were discontinued, by his untimely death. George Floyd, as the deceased, would need help adjusting to his own loss. Former NBA star Stephen Jackson was one of those bereaved by his death. They had been friends from childhood, and Jackson described Floyd as his "twin" brother. In his grief, Jackson told Floyd's young daughter Gianna, "I'll walk you down the aisle one day" (https://www.tmz.com /2020/06/02/stephen-jackson-mlb-nfl-owners-nba-justice-george -floyd-video/). Jackson, in his grief, placed attention on his deceased friend, and in helping Floyd to adjust to his loss promised to be an extension of Floyd's legs, arms, eyes, and ears in the world of the living. This promise and similar others made to Gianna would be pleasing to Floyd, who according to Ancestor worshippers is aware of happenings in the world of the living. In return, Jackson would be able to receive satisfaction and healing to his grief. The intrinsic benefits from pleasing others is further discussed in a later chapter.

Key Terms

Ancestral heritage
Continuing bond
Deceased-focused approach
Dual bereavement adjustment
Memorial
Modernization
Proper burial
Symbolic actions
Traditional religious practices
Western burials

SUMMARY

1. Christianity is the dominant religion in South America. However, based on ancestral heritage practitioners of other religions abound, as well; and the practice of Christianity is combined with other religions in death and dying rituals and beliefs. In some cases, Christian practices are akin to traditional religious practices in symbols.
2. Among certain groups (e.g., Afro-Surinamese), grief resolution occurs when the deceased person is given a "proper" burial in accordance with traditions and norms.
3. The **deceased-focused model** is a proposed alternative to adjusting to a loss. The bereaved is healed when the needs of the deceased are also met, with the deceased being the focus of attention.

Review Questions

1. How is the **deceased-focused approach to mourning** different from other grief models?
2. Do you know of someone who has acted in ways that are pleasing to a deceased loved one? How would you describe their feelings doing such?
3. Can maintaining continuing bond with the deceased person help or hurt the bereaved?
4. What is your preference: maintaining continuing bond or not?
5. What would a "proper" burial be in Western and non-Western cultures?
6. Are you aware of Christian practices that are similar to traditional religious practices?
7. What would be your choice of a memorial that could also become a continuing bond with the deceased?

Additional Readings

Gooren, H. (Ed.). (2019). *Encyclopedia of Latin American religions.* Basel, Switzerland: Springer.

Will de Chaparro, M., & Achim, M. (2011). (Eds.). *Death and dying in colonial Spanish America.* Tucson, AZ: University of Arizona Press.

Chapter 7

DEATH, DYING AND BEREAVEMENT IN ASIA

Chapter Outline

Learning objectives
Life expectancy and the prevalent causes of death
Religions of Asia
Buddhism
Buddhism and other religions in China
Hinduism
Hinduism in India
Key terms
Summary
Review questions
Additional readings

Learning Objectives

LO1: Explain the different levels of development of the countries in Asia

LO2: Discuss the predominant causes of death of countries in Asia

LO3: Describe death, dying and bereavement practices and beliefs that reflect on Collectivism

LO4: Explain death, dying and bereavement practices and beliefs based on Hinduism

LO5: Understand death, dying and bereavement practices and beliefs based on Buddhism

LO6: Describe death, dying and bereavement practices and beliefs based on Taoism

Figure 7.1
Map of Asia

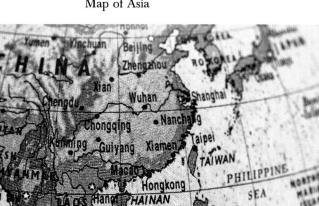

Source: Istockphoto.com

LIFE EXPECTANCY AND PREVALENT CAUSES OF DEATH

Asia is the world's largest and most populous continent. The countries in Asia that also have land masses in Europe include Russia, Turkey, Georgia, Azerbaijan and Kazakhstan. And Yemen, another country in Asia, is part of the Middle East. These nations are not included in the list of countries in Figure 7.2. In Figure 7.2, there are six countries that have life expectancy of 80 years and older and 10 others that have life expectancy below 70 years, showing a significant variance in life expectancy in the Asian region.

Japan has the highest life expectancy at 85.30 years and Afghanistan has the lowest at 51.70 years. Afghanistan's conflicts from a series of wars starting in 1978 might have contributed to its relatively low life expectancy. The World Bank (2020) lists Afghanistan as a

Figure 7.2
Life Expectancy of Countries in Asia, 2017

Country	Life Expectancy (in years)
Japan	85.30
Singapore	85.20
Macau	84.60
Hong Kong	83.00
South Korea	82.50
Taiwan	80.20
Brunei	77.30
Sri Lanka	76.90
Maldives	75.80
China	75.70
Malaysia	75.20
Thailand	74.90
Uzbekistan	74.00
Vietnam	73.70
Bangladesh	73.40
Indonesia	73.00
Nepal	71.00
Kyrgyzstan	70.90
North Korea	70.70
Bhutan	70.60
Turkmenistan	70.40
Mongolia	69.90

continued

Figure 7.2—*Continued*

Country	Life Expectancy (in years)
Philippines	69.40
India	68.80
Timor Leste	68.40
Myanmar	68.20
Pakistan	68.10
Tajikistan	68.10
Cambodia	64.90
Laos	64.60
Afghanistan	51.70

Source: CIA Factbaook, n.d.; https://www.cia.gov/library/publications/the-world-factbook/rankorder/2102rank.html)

low income economy and the predominant causes of death in such societies include communicable diseases such as diarrheal diseases, HIV/AIDS, and tuberculosis. Other prevalent causes of death include preterm birth complications, birth asphyxia and birth trauma, and road injury.

RELIGIONS OF ASIA

The continent of Asia has numerous religions, but the dominant ones are Islam, Hinduism, Buddhism, Sikhism and Christianity. The vast majority of practitioners of Hinduism (99%) and Buddhism (99%) reside in Asia with over 1 billion practitioners in both China (1.386 billion) and India (1.339 billion) (e.g., Pew Research, 2012; https://www.pewforum.org/2012/12/18/global-religious-landscape-exec/). Whereas Buddhism has the largest following in China (estimated 185-250 million practitioners), Hinduism is the dominant religion of India (practiced by almost 80% of the population). The dominance of Buddhism extends to Cambodia, Thailand, Myanmar, Bhutan, Sri Lanka and Mongolia; and of Hinduism to Nepal (e.g., Pew Research, 2012). Both Buddhism and Hinduism teach rebirth of the human soul after death. Figure 7.3 provides some basic tenets of both religions.

Figure 7.3
Buddhist and Hinduist Beliefs About Death, Dying and the Afterlife

Buddhist beliefs	Hinduist beliefs
Death prospects should be faced earlier in life, so that when the time comes pain and suffering would not be a distraction (e.g., Masel, Schur & Watzke, 2012)	Death is a transition to another life; believe in reincarnation
There is no separation between body and soul and there is none among entities of the world. This interconnection is in constant change (e.g., Masel, Schur & Watzke, 2012)	There is good rebirth (or reincarnation) caused by good karma and bad rebirth caused by bad karma. A person's good or bad actions will result in good or bad karma (e.g., Lipner, 2012; Sharma et al., 2013).
Humans are housed in a body but do not own the body (e.g., Masel, Schur & Watzke, 2012)	Suffering is related to Karma (e.g., Thrane, 2010)
There are Four Noble Truths: 1) that life is about suffering, pain and misery; 2) that suffering, pain and misery are the result of selfish desires; 3) that you can overcome suffering either in this life or in the afterlife by achieving Nirvana (a transcendental state devoid of suffering, pleasure or desires); and 4) that knowledge about the unsatisfactory nature of life leads to having the right mindset and actions, thereby not subject to	Death is not a contradiction of life, and neither is life a contradiction of death; both occur in a cyclical manner (e.g., Hinduismtoday.com, n.d.; https://www.hinduismtoday.com/modules/smartsection/item.php?itemid=1667)

continued

Figure 7.3—*Continued*

Buddhist beliefs	Hinduist beliefs
suffering (e.g., Britannica. Com, n.d.) https://www.britannica.com /topic/Four-Noble-Truths)	
Meditation on the Four Noble truths enables the human mind to exercise control over the body, in the process of dying	Cremation is preferred over earth burial for quicker release of the spirit
Detachment from suffering requires a Noble Eightfold Pathway (e.g., Puchalski & O'Donnell, 2005): —right intention —right understanding —right speech —right action —right living —right mindfulness —right effort —right concentration	Funerals serve a dual purpose: 1) to notify the spirit of the deceased it no longer belongs to the body of the deceased so as not to linger around; and 2) for the family to say farewell to the deceased and to express their grief and loss (e.g., Hinduismtoday.com; https://www .hinduismtoday.com/modules /smartsection/item.php?itemid=1667)

Source: Author's creation.

Buddhism

Narrating the story of a cancer patient with a severe pain, Eva Masel and colleagues (2012) pointed to the impact that the teachings of Buddhism had on a Christian patient, who was visited by a Buddha master. After the Buddhist master told her not to think about how long her pain would last but to admit that *this* is pain (which the world is about), the patient was able to handle the pain with that perspective in mind. In effect, the Buddhist master is able to get the patient into a state of Nirvana which is a transcendental state devoid of suffering or self-desires.

Buddhism and Other Religions in China

China is a country with a confluence of religions. Whereas Buddhism is practiced by 18.2% (approximately 244 million) of the population, there is an admixture of long-held practices and beliefs in Confucius, Daoism and Ancestor worship which helps to shape the Chinese beliefs about death and dying (e.g., Hsu, O'Connor & Lee, 2009). In the Confucius belief system life and death are interconnected. Death marks another phase of life; but what determines the nature of life after death is how life is lived here on earth. Therefore, the focus should be on living a life in which good use is put into one's time here on earth (e.g., Hsu et al., 2009).

In Taoism, there is emphasis on balance, and each individual should strive to achieve this balance in their personal life. Poor balance (poor feng-shui) or lack of balance between humans and nature could lead to ill health or death. This concept of balance extends to the elements of the universe, also. Death is understood as the balance to life and not necessarily an achievement or graduation from life (e.g., Kleeman, 2003; Lo, 1999). Therefore, efforts to prolong life through medicine are not discouraged. Taoists also believe in a relationship between the living and the dead (e.g., Kemp & Chang, 2002). Among the Chinese practitioners of Ancestor worship the burial of an elderly person is treated with respect, and with proper traditional rituals which include choosing the right day and location for burial, burning symbolic paper money, and lighting up candles at ceremonies in memory of the deceased (e.g., Braun & Nichols, 1997).

Chinese Buddhism (also known as Mahayana Buddhism) is an amalgamation of Chinese traditional values of filial piety and Ancestor worship. It believes in the importance of the dying person's last thoughts as influencing that person's rebirth prospects, either good or bad (e.g., Jing Yin, 2006). Therefore, reciting of Sutra (statement of beliefs) prior to death helps the dying person's mind to stay focused on paradise (e.g., Hsieh, 2002; Hsu et al., 2009). However, afterlife beliefs may not be a buffer against death anxiety for everyone. A study of 141 older adult practitioners of Hong Kong Chinese Buddhism revealed that personal death anxiety was not reduced by thoughts about reincarnation, which was perceived as a renewal of suffering (e.g., Hui & Coleman, 2012).

During funerals, as a sign of good luck and happiness, the bereaved wears white or black but also red, in the case of an elderly person who has lived a long life. The deceased person is not sent to the other world empty-handed; he or she is buried with something of value like expensive jewelry or of significance to the deceased, including burial in the deceased's hometown. Such actions are perceived as pleasing to the deceased, because the belief is that if the deceased is unhappy, there would be negative consequences to the living (e.g., Kemp & Chang, 2002). In Western societies, the choice of a burial location might reflect the convenience of the survivor, especially if the death was unexpected or the deceased failed to provide a prior indication of where she or he would like to be buried. The choice of burial location may be influenced by where most family members can conveniently visit the gravesite of the deceased, including during Memorial Day celebrations.

In Chinese culture it is not appropriate to have entertainments within the first 100 days following a burial. Also, family members should expect the spirit of the deceased to visit them, especially within 3 days following a burial. Celebrations come after the 100-day period, and in the 1st and 3rd year anniversary events honoring the memory of the deceased. Two key elements that help family members go through the grieving process are family and rituals (e.g., Qin & Xia, 2015). Death brings the family together and family provides strength and support to members who see the need to be closer and tighter as their numbers dwindle by one or more than one, as in cases of multiple losses caused by the COVID-19 pandemic. The ritual of making up for an apology or appreciation owed to the deceased is never too late. It is another way to say "sorry" or "thank you," according to Shen Qin and colleague Yan Xia (2015). In Taoism, this would be the equivalence of achieving balance in order to experience peace and wholeness. The Chinese avoid mentioning "death," as it is a word they associate with bad luck, and children are usually discouraged from asking questions about death (e.g., Chan & Chow, 2006).

Hinduism

In Hinduism, a dying person tries to complete his or her "unfinished" business in order to achieve a good death. The unfinished business is not so much about personal uncompleted projects such as writing a book, but about doing good deeds, offering apology, reconciling differences, executing one's own will including distributing of properties to heirs or charities. If unfinished businesses are not resolved it will take another lifetime to undo a bad karma (e.g., Firth, 2005). Once an unfinished business is taken care of, the focus of the ailing or dying person is on God, awaiting a good rebirth. Unlike Christianity where emphasis is on accepting Christ as savior and repentance of past sins, Hinduists give special consideration to doing good deeds prior to death. Therefore, a conscious death is preferred over an unconscious death, and an expected death over an unexpected death (e.g., murder, or accident) (e.g., Firth, 2005). Elisabeth Kubler-Ross's (1969) five stages of dying did not address the issue of unfinished business, which is brought into sharper focus by Hinduism.

Home is the preferred location for dying, which allows family members (including children) to participate in dying rituals performed by a priest or an elderly family member (if a priest is not available). Dying rituals include placing the dying person in his or her own room, or in the house's entryway, with the head facing East. With a lamp lit near the head, the dying person is encouraged to say his or her mantra to encourage concentration. Loved ones read scripture, sing hymns and keep vigil until the dying person departs. Hinduists believe that it is more appealing to face death with a clear conscious mind than to be clouded by medication (e.g., Sharma, et al, 2013). Thus, mind-altering medications like narcotics are believed to alter the rebirth process (e.g., Bauer-Wu, Barrett & Yeager, 2007).

After death, the body is not embalmed and pictures on walls and mirrors are covered. The deceased person's body is dressed in a white cloth and the widow places around the deceased's neck her wedding pendant, signifying her enduring connection to him. Excessive mourning for the dead is discouraged, as too much emotional display is believed to prevent the deceased's spirit from departing. Among the Hindu Bali (a providence of Indonesia), crying for the deceased is regarded as shameful (e.g., Hinduismtoday.com, n.d.). However, in William Worden's (2008) second task of mourning the bereaved is encouraged to feel the pain of the loss (not necessarily in an expressive way). In the Hindu Bali's mourning culture, attention is given to making sure that the deceased is taken care of before attending to the needs of the bereaved. Proper burial rituals are conducted prior to or after death in order to avoid negative consequences. Researcher Shirley Firth (2005) narrates an incident involving a Hindu family whose doctors switched off a life support machine of a dying aunt and would not allow them to administer any last rites. Generations later, before engaging in any social activities such as a wedding, the family would perform those rites to seek penance to avoid any calamity.

Hindus believe in a supreme being with whom they profess a relationship in guiding them with wisdom, within the context of the cycle of life and death. To make spiritual progress, however, the cycle of death and rebirth would have to be broken (known as *Moksha*). As Firth (2005) puts it, by the grace of the supreme being, only the virtuous ones can obtain liberation from *samsara* (the cycle of birth and rebirth) and go to heaven; or as Sharma et al. (2013) would suggest are absorbed into Brahma (ultimate reality).

Hinduism in India

Hinduism is practiced by most people in India (about 80% of the population) (e.g., The Hindu, 2006; https://www.thehindu.com/news /national/religious-communities-census-2011-what-the-numbers-say /article7582284.ece). Practitioners of the religion have an interesting custom called Sati, which is pervasive in the rural areas, although banned by the government. In Sati (meaning virtuous woman), a widow chooses to die with her husband during cremation by jumping into the funeral pyre. A case happened in an Indian village where Charan Shah, a widow, took her life by jumping into her deceased husband's funeral pyre. Government officials called her action one of suicide stemming from illiteracy, prejudice and disease. Yet, fellow Hinduists applauded her action, with thousands visiting the village where the event took place. According to locals, Charan Shah was deemed as carrying out a "wifely duty" by immolating herself (Mukerjee, 1999; https://www.latimes.com/archives/la-xpm-1999-dec-26-mn-47664-story.html).

Paul Watson (2002) of the Los Angeles Times reported on the plight of some widows who decided to not commit sati. Rather they moved close to the Ganges River, believing that death by the banks of the holy river would reunite them with their creator and break the cycle of birth, death and reincarnation. And with this liberation infinite distress is taken away, a situation known as *moksha*. For this same purpose Paul Watson (2002) also reported the accounts of social workers who disclose that between 2,000 and 5,000 impoverished widows moved from other parts of the country to the city of Varanasi, to be close to the Ganges River. The thoughts of dying by the banks of the Ganges

River in order to achieve *moksh*, brings comfort and liberation to widows. In Hinduism, the Ganges River is treated with reverence and a sprinkle of its water is believed to impart purity on a person
(Mukerjee, 1999; https://www.latimes.com/archives/la-xpm-2002-nov-24-fg-widows24-story.html). Hindu tradition bars remarriage for widows, who most times are uneducated with few skills and financial support. The Hindu Widows' Remarriage Act of 1856 did legalize remarriage for Hindu windows (e.g., Parashar, 2008). However, as with sati, collectivist actions do override individualism in remarriage decisions. In Hinduism (and Buddhism), the focus is on how life on earth should be lived in order to have a good life on earth and in the afterlife. This orientation is however different from Ancestor worship where the type of relationship maintained between the living and the dead is more important.

Key Terms

Ancestor worship
Balance
Buddhism
Chines Buddhism
Chinese Traditional values
Confucius beliefs
Ganges River
Sati
"Unfinished" business

SUMMARY

1. Asia is the world's largest and most populous continent. It has six countries with life expectancy above 80 years, with Japan as the highest (at 85.30 years). Ten countries have life expectancy below 70 years, with Afghanistan as the lowest (at 51.70 years).
2. Asia has numerous religions, but Islam, Hinduism, Buddhism Sikhism and Christianity are the dominant ones. The continent has the vast majority of practitioners of Hinduism (99%) and Buddhism (99%). Whereas Buddhism has the largest following in China (estimated 185-250 million practitioners), Hinduism is

the dominant religion of India (practiced by almost 80% of the population).

3. Chinese Buddhism (also known as Mahayana Buddhism) is an amalgamation of Chinese traditional values of filial piety and Ancestor worship. It believes in the importance of last thoughts of a dying person—which will influence that person's rebirth prospects, either good or bad. Thus, reciting the Sutra (statement of beliefs) prior to death helps the dying person's mind to stay focused on paradise.

4. In Hinduism, to complete "unfinished" business is to achieve good death. The unfinished business may be about doing good deeds, offering apology, reconciling differences, executing one's own will such as distributing properties to heirs or charities. If unfinished business is not resolved it will take another lifetime to undo a bad karma. Once unfinished business is taken care of, focus should be on God, in awaiting a good rebirth.

Review Questions

1. What are the similarities and differences between Buddhism and Hinduism?
2. What elements are involved in death and dying practices of Chinese Buddhism?
3. The practice of Sati by widows in India is banned by the government, yet heralded by the locals, especially in rural areas. What is an alternative available to widows?
4. Why is a "conscious" death preferred over an "unconscious" death in Hinduism?
5. How is the practice of Buddhism or Hinduism different from Ancestor worship in afterlife beliefs?

Additional Readings

Chee-Kiong, T. (2012). *Chinese death rituals in Singapore*. Abington, UK: Routledge.

Nadeau, R. L. (2014). *Asian religions: A cultural perspective*. Hoboken, NJ: Wiley-Blackwell Publishing.

Chapter 8

DEATH, DYING AND
BEREAVEMENT IN EUROPE

Chapter Outline

Learning objectives
Life expectancy and the prevalent causes of death
Influence of Christianity and other belief systems in death and dying
    practices
Superstitious beliefs
Modernization
Estonia
Romania
Italy
Traditional beliefs
Key terms
Summary
Review questions
Additional readings

Learning Objectives

LO1: Understand levels of religiosity of the countries in Europe
LO2: Understand life expectancy for countries in Europe
LO3: Comprehend the top killer diseases/factors in Europe
LO4: Explain the role of superstitions in death, dying and bereavement practices
LO5: Understand death, dying and bereavement beliefs and practices in Estonia

LO6: Describe death, dying and bereavement beliefs and practices in Romania

LO7: Explain death, dying and bereavement beliefs and practices in Italy

LIFE EXPECTANCY AND PREVALENT CAUSES OF DEATH

Figure 8.2 presents the life expectancy for countries in Europe. Several of the countries have life expectancy at 80 years or above. The World Bank (2020) classifies most of the nations as either upper-middle income or high-income countries. As mentioned in earlier chapters, upper-middle income and high-income economies have non-commu-

Figure 8.1
Map of Europe

Source: Istockphoto.com

nicable diseases making up the top 10 killer factors, whereas lower income countries have communicable diseases as prevalent causes of death (e.g., lower respiratory infections).

Figure 8.2
Life Expectancy of Countries in Europe, 2017

Country	Life Expectancy (in years)
Monaco	89.40
San Marino	83.30
Iceland	83.10
Switzerland	82.60
Italy	82.30
Lixembourg	82.30
Sweden	82.10
Liechtenstein	81.90
Norway	81.90
France	81.90
Spain	81.80
Austria	81.60
Netherlands	81.40
Belgium	81.10
Finland	81.00
Ireland	80.90
Germany	80.80
United Kingdom	80.80
Greece	80.70
Malta	80.50

continued

Figure 8.2–*Continued*

Country	Life Expectancy (in years)
Denmark	79.50
Portugal	79.40
Cyprus	78.80
Czech Republic	78.80
Albania	78.50
Slovenia	78.30
Poland	77.80
Slovakia	77.30
Estonia	76.90
Bosnia and Herzegovina	76.90
Macedonia	76.40
Croatia	76.10
Hungary	76.10
Serbia	75.70
Romania	75.40
Turkey	75.00
Lithuania	75.00
Bulgaria	74.70
Latvia	74.70
Belarus	73.00
Kazakhstan	71.00
Ukraine	72.10
Russia	71.00

Source: CIA: The World Factbook; https://www.cia.gov/library/publications/the-world-factbook/rankorder/2102rank.html)

INFLUENCE OF CHRISTIANITY AND OTHER
BELIEF SYSTEMS IN DEATH AND DYING PRACTICES

In Europe, Christianity is the dominant religion with influences on death, dying and bereavement practices. Non-Christian practices are present as well, due to superstitions or Anglo-Saxon heathenism or pre-Christian practices of between 5th and 8th centuries AD, including beliefs in magic and witchcraft, that have persisted over the years. Technological advancements and modernization influences have had an impact on death, dying and bereavement practices as well.

Superstitious Beliefs

The *Merriam-Webster Dictionary* (n.d.; https://www.merriam-webster.com/dictionary/superstition) defines *superstition* as a belief based on chance, fear of the unknown, magic, or false conception of causation. In Russian physiologist cum psychologist Ivan Pavlov's (1977) Classical Conditioning Theory, superstition could be a learned response. In his experiment with dogs, Pavlov noted that a naturally occurring stimulus such as food (unconditioned stimulus) gave rise to a naturally occurring response such as salivation (unconditioned response). However, when paired closely in time (e.g., a fraction of seconds) with food, a bell (conditioned stimulus) also elicited salivation (a conditioned response). In other words, salivating to a bell (which is not food) is a learned response. Similarly, in explaining death causation, a learned response could occur, also. For example, a person died of a sudden cardiac arrest and is medically proven through an autopsy report. However, just prior to the incident he or she had visited a family member believed to be jealous of the deceased person. The death causation may be explained as resulting from the jealous relative's "evil eye," irrespective of a medical autopsy report to the contrary. In many cultures around the world, evil eye is believed to be a curse or a malevolent glare to cause injury or destruction (e.g., Ross, 2010). In the UK, some superstitions about death and dying include the direction of burial for the deceased, whether East or West. With paganism, East reflects the rising sun, and, therefore, in the afterlife the deceased is expected to rise just like the sun. Also, the eyelids of the deceased are covered because a dead person could cause misfortune to a living person if looked at (a reverse evil eye). A misfortunate that befell the person who "looked at" the deceased person would be attributed to the incident. Sometimes, pennies are used to keep the dead person's eyes shut. In ancient Greece and Rome, however, pennies are used for different purposes. They are placed inside the deceased's mouth to pay the ferryman, Charon, to allow the dead person's spirit to cross the Styx river (a deity and river in Greek mythology) into the afterlife. In 17th century Wales, pennies are placed in the mouth of the deceased to give money "to St. Peter." Thus, as money enables access in the world of the living, so would it be in the world of the dead. Also, in a dead person's house, mirrors are covered because the dead person's soul is believed to be trapped in the mirror. If you saw yourself in that mirror, you would join the deceased shortly after (e.g., History.co.uk, n.d.; https://www.history.co.uk/history-of-death /death-rituals-and-superstitions).

Modernization

Modernization (the transformation of lives based on industrialization and technology) has helped in reducing superstitious beliefs, especially in the urban centers. Modernization has led to the reduction of religious practices, as well. Church funeral is declining and instead the preference is to have memorial ceremonies and burial practices that reflect the individual's choice, e.g., burial at sea, sprinkling of cremated ashes from the sky, or in fireworks. There is also the use of technology and digital media to webcast or livestream funerals. Increasingly, there is the tendency to treat the memory of the deceased as separate from the lifeless body of the deceased (e.g., Richardson, 2000). Memorial events are held to remember the deceased with more people participating even on social media, whereas the occasion of the final act on the dead body (which includes burial, donation to science or cremation) attracts less attendance and may be limited to close family members, only.

While modernization has led to the decline of religious practices in Europe, it has also put into sharper focus the desire to embrace traditional practices and beliefs on death and dying, especially in the rural areas. As shown in Figure 8.3, a Pew Research study (2018; https: //www.pewresearch.org/fact-tank/2018/12/05/how-do-european -countries-differ-in-religious-commitment/) of 34 countries in Europe shows a continent where religious practices are on the decline.

Figure 8.3
Percentage of Adults Who Are "Highly Religious"

Country	Percentage of people who are "highly Religious"
Romania	55
Armenia	51
Georgia	50
Greece	49
Moldova	47
Bosnia	46
Croatia	44
Poland	40
Portugal	37
Serbia	32
Ukraine	31
Slovakia	29
Belarus	27
Italy	27
Ireland	24
Lithuania	21
Spain	21
Bulgaria	18
Netherland	18
Hungary	17
Norway	17
Russia	17
Latvia	15
Austria	14

continued

Figure 8.3—*Continued*

Country	Percentage of people who are "highly Religious"
Finland	13
France	12
Germany	12
Switzerland	12
United Kingdom	11
Belgium	10
Sweden	10
Czech Republic	8
Denmark	8
Estonia	7

Source: Pew Research Center, 2018; https://www.pewresearch.org/fact-tank/2018/12/05/how-do-european-countries-differ-in-religious-commitment/

The Pew Research study (2018) used four measures to define "highly religious" individuals, with high observance in at least two of them: a) attending religious services at least monthly; b) praying at least daily; c) believing in God with absolute certainly; and d) saying that religion is very important to them. If, however, a person's observance is low on one measure (e.g., seldom or never attending religious services) but high on the other three he or she is still considered highly religious.

Only three countries have highly religious adults at 50% or above (Romania, Armenia and Georgia). Half of the countries surveyed (seventeen) have percentages below 20% of highly religious adults. Italy, the seat of the Roman Catholic church with a worldwide following of 2.1 billion people, is at 27%.

ESTONIA

Estonia has the lowest percentage of highly religious adults at only seven percent as shown in Figure 8.3. In the rural areas especially, death and dying practices are influenced by superstitious beliefs. For example, there is a belief about a good and a bad time to die. A good time to die is spring when new leaves appear on trees or autumn when trees shed their leaves. These times, including the opening of a door or window, are believed to make the journey of a departing soul easier. On the contrary, a blizzard or a storm is when evil people are believed to die (e.g., Estonica.org, n.d.; http://www.estonica.org/en /Culture/Traditional_folk_culture/Death/). As illustrated in Figure 8.4, burial practices reflect a need to protect both the living from the dead and make the dead person's transition to the afterlife easier (Heapost, 2007).

Figure 8.4
Practices that Protect both the Living from the Dead and
Make Transition of the Dead to the Afterlife Easier

Practices to protect the living from the dead	Practices believed to make transition to the afterlife easier
Place soap/bath whisk used to wash the dead body in the coffin	Open the door or window of the house in which there is a dead person
Pour water used to wash dead body in a place where nobody goes	Include small tools in the coffin, e.g., knives, needles, whetstones, fire steels
Remove nothing from the house while the dead body is still in the house as it might cause accidents	Include utensils in the coffin
Burn the bear or ladder on which the dead body is washed	Include body or personal care items in the coffin e.g., brush, comb, soap, handkerchief

continued

Figure 8.4—*Continued*

Practices to protect the living from the dead	Practices believed to make transition to the afterlife easier
Sweep clean or fumigate the room where the dead body was kept	Include nourishments in the coffin, e.g., food
Relatives do not dig the grave	Include items for social activities in the coffin e.g., alcohol, tobacco
After burial, the memory of the departed is celebrated by slaughtering an animal. If not, animals would die and the departed would return to haunt the living. Leftover food is poured on the ground to honor the departed	Include spending money in the coffin e.g., coin

Source: Author's creation.

Estonians believe that life continues in the afterlife, a place where only the dead belongs. They also believe that the dead can visit the living from the afterlife. When the dead visits the world of the living, it is usually to signal a disappointment (e.g., when a ritual was omitted during burial) with grave consequences to the living. They also believe that it is important to situate and prepare the deceased for the life to come during burial. Therefore, a range of items is included in the dead person's coffin. In a study of three southeastern districts of Estonia, researcher Torp-Koivupuu (2003) noted from the respondents surveyed that 39.3% reported including favorite items of the deceased in the coffin, 33.9% mentioned coins, and 23.2% named a bottle of vodka as grave gifts. Also, forgotten items that are not included in the coffin are brought to the cemetery and buried by the grave (e.g., Valk, 2006). It should be noted that grave gifts usually reflect the dead person's wishes or what would be pleasing to the deceased. The living creates an image of the afterworld based on their understanding of the world in which they live. However, in the world of the living, the living exists in a bodily form, whereas in the world of the dead, the dead exists in spirit form. Unlike the living, however, in spirit form the deceased has the flexibility to assume multiple states, and when visiting the world of the living, the deceased could choose to take the form of a bird or a butterfly (e.g., Loorits, 1949). Communication between the living and the dead is verbal (e.g., talking to the dead), but it could also be non-verbal such as appeasing the deceased through foods and drinks (e.g., Valk, 2006).

ROMANIA

According to the Pew Research Center's (2018) survey, Romania is at 55% of highly religious adults. Irrespective of a relatively high percentage of religiosity (compared to other countries), Romania's current death customs and rituals are based on ancient Romanian mythologies (e.g., Mihaela, 2015). According to Romanian mythology, based on pagan beliefs the soul leaves the deceased person and integrates with the universe after death.

The ease with which the soul leaves the body would depend on the level of morality of the deceased person. For example, it is easier for the soul of a child without sin to depart to the other world. Also, prayers said by a priest on a dying person are believed to facilitate the passing of the soul from the body. About three days (and sometimes up to 40 days) after the soul departs the body, it is believed that the spirit lingers around where the dead person lived.

In preparation for burial the body is bathed and dressed and laid in a coffin with a candle lit. The light from the candle is to help guide the soul now surrounded by darkness into the life beyond. November 21st, called *Ovidenie,* is a day to light a candle and is set apart for people who die suddenly (e.g., suicide) and considered to die without a candle (e.g., Mihaela, 2015). The wake lasts about three days and the priest is invited to come and perform rituals, including readings from the Bible taken from the four gospels, blessing the burial feast and splashing the coffin with wine and oil. The dead person's clothes and other items that are considered useful in the other world are given out to the poor. Burial feasts to commemorate the deceased person's death occurs after a week, a month, 3 months, 6 months and a year. Subsequently, this continues at least once a year for the next 7 years.

The Romanian pagan tradition recognizes many gods made up of the souls of dead relatives that could influence the living, for better or for worse. During grieving, actions that portray respect for the dead include: men wearing their caps for 40 days, not cutting their hair nor shaving, and women taking their skull caps off and girls letting their hair down. Also, the dead is commemorated on the Holy Thursday of the Holy week during which people wake up at 4 am, light fires in front of their houses and then go to the cemetery and pay their respects and ask the dead person to come back to this world and see what has happened to their families (e.g., Mihaela, 2015). Alongside the traditional beliefs and practices, practitioners of Christianity believe that people who accept Christ as savior prior to death are united with him in heaven and are victorious over death. In both traditional and Christian beliefs, Romanians accept the afterlife in various forms but do not believe in reincarnation. As mentioned earlier, the renaissance of traditional beliefs and practices in death and dying practices may relate to the general decline of Christianity in Europe, even for Romania with a relatively high percentage (55%) of highly religious adults, according to the Pew Research Center's (2018) survey.

ITALY

Italy is the headquarters of the Catholic faith, a religion with a global reach of 1.2 billion people (e.g., BBC; 2013; https://www.bbc.com/news/world-21443313). Expectedly, Italian funerals are influenced by the Roman Catholic teachings that include beliefs in heaven, hell or purgatory. Also, in burials there is the invocation of the Holy Trinity of God the Father, Jesus the Son, and the Holy Spirit in guiding the deceased's loved ones. Prayers are said during vigil and wake, and the Rosary is prayed personally lasting up to 20 minutes. A funeral mass is held at the church prior to burial at a cemetery. Prior to death, a priest is called to administer the last rites to a dying person to ease passage into the afterlife (Sekulska, 2019; https://www.joincake.com/blog/italian-funeral/).

Traditional Beliefs

Alongside Catholic rituals, there are traditional belief systems that guide death, dying and bereavement practices, as well. In Italian folk belief the spirit of the deceased should be appeased as the spirit is able to hear, see or taste. If not, the dead person's spirit can come back to haunt the living. Offerings are left for the soul of the deceased, who is believed to come out at night on the Day of the Dead. Deceased persons are also buried with their favorite items such as cigarettes. Italians are either appeasing the soul of the dead or taking measures to stop it from visiting the living. They spread salt around the house and on the chest of the deceased to prevent the spirit from visiting the living because the deceased is perceived as unwilling to journey into the afterlife.

After burial, family and friends take a different route back home in order to confuse the soul and prevent it from following them. The spirits of dead children are also both pacified and prevented from visiting the living. At the Cemetery of the Babies (or *La Necropoli dei Bambini*) such items as puppies and animal bones to pacify and stones to weigh down the hands and feet of dead children to prevent them from visiting the living to haunt them have been discovered (Sekulska, 2019; https://www.joincake.com/blog/italian-funeral/). Italians demonstrate a dual belief system in death, dying and bereavement practices—also known as accommodation behavior.

Key Terms

Christianity
Estonia
Highly religious adults
Italy
Modernization
Non-Christian practices
Pagan tradition
Romania
Superstition

SUMMARY

1. There is a decline in religiosity in Europe. In a 2018 Pew research survey of 34 countries in Europe, only three countries have highly religious adults at 50% or above (Romania, Armenia and Georgia). Half of the countries surveyed (seventeen) have percentages below 20% of highly religious adults. Italy, the seat of the Roman Catholic church with a following of 2.1 billion

people worldwide, is at 27%. Four measures define "highly religious" individuals, with high observance in at least two of them: a) attending religious services at least monthly, b) praying at least daily, c) believing in God with absolute certainly, and d) saying that religion is very important to them. If a person's observance is low on one measure (e.g., seldom or never attending religious services), but high on the other three, he or she is still considered highly religious.

2. The declines in religiosity might create a void in death, dying and bereavement practices for traditional beliefs and practices (and modernization influences) to flourish. Estonians, for example, believe that the dead can visit the living. When the dead visits the world of the living, it is usually to signal a disappointment (e.g., when a ritual was omitted during burial). And this has grave consequences for the living. Therefore, they prepare the deceased for the life to come by having his or her favorite items included in the coffin.

3. The Romanians believe that after death the soul leaves the dead person and integrates with the universe. The ease with which the soul leaves the body would depend on the level of morality of the deceased person. They also believe that after the soul departs the body, it hovers around where the dead person lived for about three days (and sometimes up to 40 days).

4. Italy is the seat of the Catholic church with a global followership of 1.2 billion people. Yet Italians have a mix of Roman Catholicism and folk beliefs in death, dying and bereavement practices. Traditional practices include both appeasing the deceased and taking measures to prevent the spirit of the deceased from visiting the living.

Review Questions

1. Superstitions might not have scientific basis yet people believe in them. Why?
2. What do you think are the factors responsible for the decline of religiosity in Europe?
3. Are there similarities and differences in death, dying, and bereavement beliefs and practices in Estonia, Romania, and Italy?

4. What are the advantages or disadvantages of superstitious beliefs in death, dying and bereavement practices?
5. Are you aware of any superstitions in death, dying or bereavement? Do you personally believe in them and how did you learn about them?

Additional Readings

Korpiola, M., & Lahtinen, A. (Eds.). (2015). *Cultures of death and dying in mediaeval and early modern Europe.* Helsinki, Finland: Helsinki Collegium for Advanced Studies, University of Helsinki Finland.

Tarlow, S. (2011). *Ritual, belief and the dead in early modern Britain and Ireland.* Cambridge, UK: Cambridge University Press.

Chapter 9

DEATH, DYING AND BEREAVEMENT IN OCEANIA

Chapter Outline

Learning objectives
Life expectancy and the prevalent causes of death
Australia
New Zealand
Papua New Guinea
Tradition versus modernity
Reverse influence of tradition on modernity
Co-existence of tradition and modernity
Key terms
Summary
Review questions
Additional readings

Learning Objectives

LO1: Examine the life expectancy of countries in Oceania
LO2: Comprehend the predominant causes of death in Oceania
LO3: Describe the afterlife beliefs of Indigenous peoples of Australia
LO4: Explain death, dying and bereavement practices in New Zealand
LO5: Understand death, dying and bereavement practices in Papua New Guinea
LO6: Explain the co-existence of traditional and modern values and practices in death, dying and bereavement

Figure 9.1
Map of Countries Located in Oceania

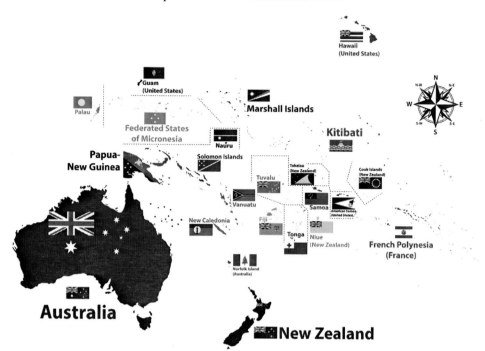

Source: Istockphoto.com

LIFE EXPECTANCY AND PREVALENT CAUSES OF DEATH

The following 14 countries make up Oceania: Australia, Fiji, Kiribati, Marshall Islands, Micronesia, Nauru, New Zealand, and Palau. Others include: Papua New Guinea, Samoa, Solomon Islands, Tonga, Tuvalu, and Vanuatu (e.g., Brittanica.com, n.d.; https://www.britannica .com/place/Pacific-Islands/Early-period). Figure 9.2 provides the range of life expectancy of countries in the region. Based on World Bank's (2020) classifications, Kiribati, Micronesia, Papua New Guinea, Solomon Islands, and Vanuatu fall under lower middle-income economies ($1,026–3,995), and the countries of Fiji, Marshall Islands, Nauru, Samoa, Tonga and Tuvalu are upper middle-income countries ($3,996–12,375). The nations of Australia, New Zealand and Palau are described as high-income economies ($12,376 or more). Most of the top 10 killer diseases or incidences responsible for death in upper middle-income and high-income economies are noncommunicable factors (e.g., heart disease, cancer). However, lower middle-income countries have prevalent causes of death from communicable diseases such as diarrheal diseases, tuberculosis, and lower respiratory infections (WHO, 2018).

Figure 9.2
Life Expectancy of Countries in Oceania, 2017

Country	**Life Expectancy (in years)**
Australia	82.30
New Zealand	81.30
Tonga	76.40
Solomon Islands	75.60
Samoa	74.00
Vanuatu	73.70
Marshall Islands	73.40
Palau	73.40
Micronesia	73.10
Fiji	73.00
Nauru	67.40
Papua New Guinea	67.30
Tuvalu	66.90
Kiribati	66.50

Source: CIA: Factbook; https://www.cia.gov/library/publications/the-world-factbook /rankorder/2102rank.html)

AUSTRALIA

With a population projected at 25.6 million in 2020, Australia is the largest country in Oceania, with Sidney as both the nation's capital and the region's largest city (e.g., https://www.abs.gov.au/ausstats /abs%40.nsf/94713ad445ff1425ca25682000192af2/1647509ef7e25 faaca2568a900154b63?OpenDocument; Population Clock, June 2020). The prevalent cause of death in 2010 is heart disease (e.g., Australian Bureau of Statistics, 2010; https://www.abs.gov.au/ausstats/abs@.nsf /Products/6BAD463E482C6970CA2579C6000F6AF7?opendocument), and as with other Western developed nations, most Australians die in the hospital. After death, the deceased's body is removed to the mortuary and the decedent's family arranges for a funeral with the help of a professional funeral director. The deceased's body is washed and prepared for burial or cremation, and viewing is done at a funeral home, with friends and visitors coming to pay their last respects to the deceased and consoling the family.

Majority of Australians are Christians, similar to other nations of Oceania. Funeral services include prayers, hymns, storytelling and a slide show of the deceased (e.g., Jones, 2015). Cremation is the preferred choice, especially in the city, and the *cremains* (cremation ashes) are spread in places that are associated with the deceased. Earth burial takes place in cemeteries, usually with beds that have religious themes (e.g., the bed of resurrection). After cremation or earth burial loved ones, friends, and visitors gather in a multi-purpose hall or a relative's home for eating, drinking and for more storytelling (e.g., Jones, 2015).

Indigenous Australians (or Aboriginals) make up about 3.3% of Australia's population. Though ethnically diverse, some commonalities among them provide a different perspective to the mainstream Caucasian's ways of death, dying and bereavement. The Indigenous Australians believe that everything is interconnected—birth, death, the lands and elements of nature. They also believe that elders are the representatives of God who should be obeyed (e.g., Jones, 2015). The Indigenous people believe in an afterlife where the deceased joins the ancestor in spirit form and provides guidance to the living. The living engages the spirit of the departed in *ancestor listening* as opposed to Ancestor worship. Ancestors are spoken to as if they are in bodily form, but their names are never mentioned, especially during mourning—which could last up to six months, depending on the status of the deceased person in society prior to death.

As a sign of respect to the deceased and to not cause further pain to the decedent's loved ones, a person who bears the same name as the deceased would have to change his or her name. Also, personal belongings of the deceased are destroyed and people move away from the home where the deceased person had died. Indigenous people go through the pain of bereavement by avoiding physical cues that remind them of the deceased (e.g., name, personal belongness) (e.g., Jones, 2015). In bereavement, William Worden (2008) recommends that people should accept the reality of their loss; work through their pain and loss; adjust to a new environment created by their loss; and find an enduring connection to the deceased while moving forward with their lives. For Australia's Indigenous people, however, any cue (e.g., name sake of the deceased, belongings of the deceased) that would remind them of the deceased is avoided so as to not cause further pain. It appears that they perceive the stress from bereavement as a threat rather than a challenge. And *avoidance behavior* may signify a culturally appropriate way to handling bereavement stress, as opposed to the individual's choice of adjusting to the stress in his or her own way. According to researcher Kate Jones (2015), working through the pain of the loss takes a collective approach. Also known as "sorry business," it also involves the community gathering together to eat, talk and cry. Such a social support helps in easing the pain associated with a loss.

In handling perceived stress from bereavement, avoidance behavior may not be adaptive in the long run, however. It could lead to anxiety disorder. In other respects, avoidance behavior could be adaptive if it enables the individual to exercise control over his or her environment (e.g., Hofmann & Hay, 2018). For Indigenous people, avoidance behavior may be in physical form only, as they believe that in spirit form the deceased could be listened to as in "ancestor listening." This ensures continuing bond with the deceased (e.g., Klass et al., 1996).

NEW ZEALAND

With an estimated population of about five million in 2020 (https://www.stats.govt.nz/topics/population), New Zealand is also a high-income economy, according to the World Bank (2020). New Zealand's population is culturally diverse, also; the largest majority is of European descent (70%), and the largest minority are the Maoris (16.5%) (https://www.stats.govt.nz/topics/population). Christianity is the professed religion by majority of New Zealanders and this is across ethnic groups. Death and dying practices are influenced by Christian beliefs. The Maoris, however, have cultural belief patterns that are different from Christian teachings. They believe that a person's life should be in harmony with the physical and spiritual worlds. The Maoris' beliefs are enduring, even with Christian teachings and modernization influences. The Maoris believe in talking to the deceased and consider the decedent's belongings as sacred (e.g., Ngata, 2005). During funeral, the deceased's coffin is placed on the floor (on a special mattress or mat) with the foot of the coffin pointing in the direction of the door. As a sign suggesting afterlife beliefs, the deceased's coffin is surrounded by the photographs of departed relatives with whom the spirit of the deceased would keep company, as a fellow ancestor. The wider community helps with food and burial arrangements, providing both hands-on and financial support. Death affords members of the community to either repay a previous support received or to pay forward for a future support to be received (e.g., Ngata, 2005). Generally, the deceased person is made to lie in state for three days and nights before burial, during which visitors pay their last respects and give speeches. After burial, family members and visitors return to the *marai* (a complex building that surrounds a courtyard for social events). A memorial ceremony is held to mark the first year anniversary, again at the *marai*, where family members come with photos of the departed and of those gone before the deceased (e.g., Ka'ai & Higgins, 2004).

Modernization Influences

Generally, in New Zealand, there are modernization influences in death and dying practices, especially in the choice of funeral location. The church is no longer the preferred location for funerals, which now includes community and school halls, sports clubs, outdoors, and homes of family/friends of the deceased. Researcher Sally Raudon (2011) notes that about 60% of funerals take place in non-church locations. Also, the number of funerals conducted by clergy has fallen with the moving of funerals away from churches. More funerals (over 60%) are conducted by a *funeral celebrant* (a paid professional with no religious affiliation, who conducts a funeral service in accordance with the values, beliefs and lifestyle of the deceased) (e.g., Schwass, 2005).

The concept of a funeral celebrant is a reflection of a modernized society that is made up of nominal Christians (e.g., Culling & Mitchell, 2015). As opposed to a Christian clergy, a funeral celebrant helps to personalize the funeral to suit the loved ones' needs, but also to legitimize the secular values of the deceased (e.g., Schafer, 2011). Legal reasons might also be responsible for moving in the direction of a funeral celebrant. In the USA, for example, Holly Yan and Rachel Bowman (2019, CNN; https://www.cnn.com/2019/11/20/us/michigan -mom-sues-priest-for-condemning-suicide-at-funeral/index.html) reported on the mother of a teenager who took his life but sued the Catholic priest who officiated in the young man's funeral for emotional harm when he condemned her son's suicide behavior as wrong in the sight of God. The mother said as parents they were expecting an "uplifting" message about their child, instead.

While cremation is more common and is relatively cheaper, it also reflects on personal/individualistic values. New Zealand funeral services offer individuals with environmental sustainability values with eco-friendly burials without embalming, a plot dug to a depth of 1 meter (about 3.3 feet), and a rapid and non-pollutant biodegradable casket. The environmentalists view burials as a donation to the environment (Manning, 2012).

Due to distance and short notices, funerals are made possible through webcasting and livestreaming for people unable to attend. When compared to a week in the UK and several days in Scandinavian countries, in New Zealand the average wait period between death and burial is three days (e.g., Raudon, 2011). However, a "typical New Zealand funeral" involves the family with photos, drawings and mementoes placed in the coffin with the deceased. Both family and friends carry the coffin with the deceased inside to the funeral venue where several people (including children) give eulogies and refreshments are served. Afterwards, close mourners return to the family home for more food and drinks (e.g., Raudon, 2011).

PAPUA NEW GUINEA

Papua New Guinea, in 2017, is a country of about 8.3 million people (World Bank, 2018a). It has a predominantly non-White population with indigenous practices and belief systems in death, dying and bereavement. According to researcher Ryan Schram (2007) the reasons the Auhelawa tribe changed its traditional practices to accommodate Christian teachings and government ideas on burials was because it was to their benefit. The Auhewala tribal people described their traditions and customs as burdensome, time consuming, and expensive, and that their tradition and custom interrupted with a speedy return to normalcy after a burial. Ryan Schram (2007) described the case of a prominent community member whose death occurred on a Friday, which required the cancellation of a youth sports event the following Saturday. This did not go well with most of the people who later rejected cancellation of the sports event they had been looking forward to. In addition, the people felt that observance of traditional burial rites stood in the way of church attendance on Sunday.

TRADITION VERSUS MODERNITY

Tradition is how things are done and known to be done over time and passed on from generation to generation, whereas Modernity reflects on a new way of thinking, of doing things which may not be in consonance with tradition. In his theory of cognitive development Swiss psychologist Jean Piaget (1976) describes the two drivers of cognitive development: assimilation and accommodation. In assimilation, an existing cognitive framework is applied to absorb information with which the individual is already familiar (e.g., tradition), whereas in accommodation, the existing cognitive framework would have to change or expand in order to take on unfamiliar information (modernity). However, the individual would have to make the choice to either hold on to that which is familiar or traditional (assimilation) or to embrace what is unfamiliar or modern (accommodation). Other times, a third party makes the choice on behalf of the individual (e.g., a government legislation on graveyard burial as opposed to house burial).

In holding on to the same thoughts and practices over time, tradition may become a tool for defining a person's sense of self. In other words, if a person says I am a Maori, he or she is also implying that this is who "I am" and this is how "we" have done things over time. Among the Maoris, the sense of selfhood is further delineated by tribal differences. Researcher Tania Ka'ai (2004) provides the following narrative from a person of the Tuhoe tribe, as an example: "My being Maori is absolutely dependent on my history as a Tuhoe person as against being a Maori person. It seems to me there is no such thing as Maoritanga because Maoritanga is an all-inclusive term which embraces all Maori. . . . Each tribe has its own history. And it's not a history that can be shared among others" (p. 23). In the narrative, this individual rejects any aspect of modernity that questions the tradition of Tuhoe and also challenges a sense of selfhood that is weaved around the Tuhoe culture. However, certain aspects of tradition, of one's sense of self, may become a burden and allows for modernity to be welcoming, such as with the case of the Auhelawa tribe of Papua New Guinea, discussed earlier. When this happens, loyalty to tradition may yield to the influence of modernity. For example, the need to spend more time with the deceased during funerals has made embalming more accepting to the Maoris (Raudon, 2011).

REVERSE INFLUENCE OF TRADITION ON MODERNITY

Tradition can have a reverse influence on modernity, as well. People may revert to ways of the past if the present or modernity does not enhance their quality of life. In other words, modernity may serve as a reminder of what was good about the past and to yearn for tradition as a result. For example, in New Zealand White Europeans who represent modernity in their ways and beliefs have been influenced by traditional Maori practices and beliefs. The Maoris' impactful practice of talking to and about the deceased and including children in burial services and ceremonies is of note. Also, prior to the farewell service/ceremony, the Maoris take the deceased home, as they believe that it is better to keep the dead body "warm" at home with loved ones than leave it cold in a mortuary. From the following narrative, Daly (2005) notes that prior to a burial, parents take their dead babies home for a while:

> A good friend of mine had a stillborn baby eight years earlier and so I knew I could bring my baby home with me. We decided to have Sasha embalmed so we could have him at home for an extended period. . . . [He] spent the next five days at home with us, tucked up in the drawer, surrounded by soft toys and special blankets and many colourful bunches of flowers. He was read to, sung to, held by all his close family. (Daly, 2005, p. 38)

CO-EXISTENCE OF TRADITION AND MODERNITY

Tradition is not always the opposite of modernity or vice versa. They can co-exist. In embracing modernity, Indigenous people may also want to keep their tradition, as it defines who they are. Christianity which represents modernity is an important aspect to death, dying and bereavement practices among Indigenous peoples of Oceania. Christianity teaches that, as all knowing, God is aware the number of days each person is ordained to live on earth. It also believes in an afterlife and that people who accept Christ as savior prior to death go to heaven. Christians also believe that death is the result of sin, as narrated in the book of Genesis chapter 3 of the Bible. Most of New Zealand's Indigenous people profess Christianity (King, 2003), yet are believers in witchcraft as a cause of death, also. They believe in ancestors who are neither in heaven nor in hell (that Christianity professes) but exist in spirit form and participate in their daily lives, in the afterlife. Researcher Tania Ka'ai (2004) notes that in the worldview of the Maoris, the following key indicators distinguish and affect death and dying practices: tribal identity, land, importance of elders, kinship structure, culture, and spirituality.

The triarchical model of the Global, Western and non-Western environmental dimensions, as discussed in previous chapters, apply to the societies of Oceania. Death causes a separation between the living and the dead resulting in sadness, a basic emotion shared by all humans (e.g., Black & Yacoob, 1997). Among the Maoris as an expression of sadness following a loss, there is weeping and wailing (e.g., Culling & Mitchell, 2015). In New Zealand, Christian teachings and technology (representing modernity) have influences on death, dying and bereavement practices. Christian teachings on afterlife suggests that the deceased goes to either heaven or hell and Christian funerals include a religious service, officiated by a priest or a minister. As earlier mentioned, Indigenous people also profess Christianity (King, 2003). Changes brought about by technology include webcasting of funerals; and with modernization, funerals services that are personalized and presided by funeral celebrants, who legitimize the secular values and lifestyle of the deceased (e.g., Schwass, 2005). Non-Western/traditional death and dying practices persist in the face of Christianity and technological advancement/modernity (e.g., Barlow & Wineti, 1991; Ka'ai & Higgins, 2004; King, 2003). After death, a common belief is that the spirit of the deceased leaves the body and journeys to the extreme end of the North Island, Cape Reinga, and then dives into the ocean of the underworld (called Hawaiki) (e.g., Mead, 2016). This is in contrast to Christian teaching that the spirit of the deceased leaves for either heaven or hell, in a skyward direction. Researchers Culling and Mitchell (2015) note that to gain an insight into the Maori's death and dying rituals and practices about the spirit's location in the afterlife, one has to understand the Maoris' belief about water as the essence of all life (e.g., doc.govt.nz, n.d.; https://www.doc .govt.nz/about-us/statutory-and-advisory-bodies/nz-conservation -authority/publications/protecting-new-zealands-rivers/02-state-of-our -rivers/maori-values/). Thus, Indigenous peoples of Oceania display accommodation behavior by embracing both Christian and Traditional belief systems. Also, Whites exemplify accommodation behavior by incorporating aspects of the Indigenous people's culture (e.g., taking the dead home before funerals) in their death, dying and bereavement practices.

Key Terms

Accommodation
Ancestor worship
Assimilation
Auhelawa tribe
Australia
Avoidance behavior
Funeral celebrant
Indigenous Australians
Maoris
Modernity
Modernization influences
New Zealand
Papua New Guinea
Tradition
Triarchical model

SUMMARY

1. The majority of the people of Australia (largest country in Oceania), as in other nations of Oceania, are Christians. Indigenous Australians make up about 3.3% of Australia's population. They believe that everything is interconnected—birth, death, the lands, and elements of nature. The Indigenous people believe in an afterlife, where the deceased person joins the ancestors in spirit form and provides guidance to the living.

2. New Zealand's population is culturally diverse, also; the largest majority being of European descent (70%) and the largest minority being the Maoris (16.5%). Whereas the majority of New Zealanders are Christians (and death and dying practices are influenced by Christian beliefs), however, the Maoris believe in Ancestor worship and that a person's life should be in harmony with the natural, physical and spiritual worlds. Modernization influences affect death and dying practices in New Zealand. For most people the funeral location is no longer the church but includes the community and school halls, sports clubs, outdoors, and homes of family/friends of the deceased. Also, more funerals (over 60%) are conducted by a *funeral celebrant* (a paid professional without any religious affiliation). As opposed to a clergy, a funeral celebrant helps to personalize the funeral and legitimize the secular values of the deceased.

3. Both traditional values and modernity co-exist, known as accommodation behavior, and is found among Indigenous people and Whites. For example, the need to spend more time with the deceased makes embalming more acceptable to Indigenous people; and the desire to take the dead body home to keep it 'warm," rather than leave it "cold" in a mortuary prior to funerals and burial, makes this practice desirable to Whites.

Review Questions

1. How do modernization influences affect death, dying and bereavement practices in Oceania?

2. What practices of indigenous people illustrate the influence of tradition in death, dying and bereavement practices?

3. How does Piaget's assimilation and accommodation concept affect the Auhelawa's (of Papua New Guinea) tribal practices in death, dying and bereavement?
4. Is *avoidance behavior* in coping with bereavement among Australia's Indigenous people a helpful behavior?
5. Have you or anyone you are familiar with used avoidance behavior in coping with a stressful situation? How did that experience turn out?
6. Would you consider using the services of a funeral celebrant? Why and why not?
7. What are examples of accommodation behavior among Indigenous people and Whites?

Additional Readings

Strathern, A., Stewart, P. J., Carucci, L. M., Poyer, L., Feinberg, R., & Macpherson, C. (2017). *Oceania: An introduction of the cultures and identities of Pacific Islander.* Durham, NC: Carolina Academic Press.

Chapter 10

CONTRIBUTIONS TO DEATH, DYING AND BEREAVEMENT MODELS FROM AROUND THE WORLD

Chapter Outline

Learning objectives
Contributory factors to life expectancy and prevalent causes of
  death
Contributory factors to death, dying and bereavement models
Influence of religion
Impacts of individualism and collectivism
Traditional/cultural practices
Influence of modernization on traditional values
Reciprocal influence of traditional values on modernization
Accommodation behavior (combining non-Western and Western
  beliefs and values)
Motivational basis for a Deceased-focused approach to bereavement
Intrinsic versus extrinsic motivation
Key terms
Summary
Review questions
Additional readings

Learning Objectives

LO1: Understand factors likely to contribute to existing bereavement
  models
LO2: Comprehend the predominant causes of death in Oceania
LO3: Explain the Deceased-focused approach to bereavement

LO4: Explain acculturation strategies
LO5: Understand accommodation behavior in religious practices

LIFE EXPECTANCY AND PREVALENT CAUSES OF DEATH

As highlighted in previous chapters, nations across the world vary in life expectancy and in prevalent factors responsible for death. Based on the World Bank's (2020) classification, countries of the world are not at the same level of socioeconomic development, which has implications for the type of prevalent factors responsible for death in those societies. In high-income and upper middle-income countries non-communicable diseases (e.g., cancer, heart disease) are mostly responsible for death, whereas in lower middle-income and low-income countries communicable diseases (e.g., HIV/AIDS) are the predominant death-causing factors, including problems with child birth and traffic accidents. Most high-income economies are Western and developed countries, whereas most low middle-income and low-income societies are non-Western and developing countries.

However, a nation's environment, especially in non-Western/developing countries, is not homogenous due to globalization and Westernization influences. In the triarchical environment of non-Western/developing societies, the global aspect is what is common to all societies; the Western (developed) dimension is due to Westernization influences, and the non-Western component is made up of elements native to the people. When an individual interacts with both Western and non-Western elements of his or her environment, "accommodation behavior" results (e.g., accepting both Western medical autopsy report and believing in witchcraft as cause for death).

CONTRIBUTORY FACTORS TO DEATH, DYING AND BEREAVEMENT MODELS

From reviewing death, dying, and bereavement practices and beliefs across the world, existing theories and models on death, dying and bereavement can benefit from the following:

1. Influence of religion
2. Impact of individualism and collectivism

3. Traditional cultural practices
4. Influence of modernization on traditional values
5. Reciprocal influence of traditional values on modernization
6. Accommodation behavior (combining of non-western and western values and practices)

Influence of Religion

Across the world, religion has a profound impact on death, dying and bereavement practices. In some parts of the world, one religion has a pervasive impact on the people, whereas in other parts the impact comes from more than one religion—for example, whereas many Africans profess Christianity or Islam, yet they combine Christianity or Islam (foreign) with Ancestor worship (indigenous religion). Intriguingly, Ancestor worship believes in reincarnation, but Christianity or Islam does not. In Australia and other nations of Oceania, Christianity is practiced by the majority of the population, yet the Indigenous people who also profess Christianity practice other religions. Just like the Africans, as dual believers in Christianity and native religions, the Indigenous people also display accommodation behavior. Similar accommodation behavior is also exemplified in South America, in the Middle East, in North America, in Europe and in Asia. In Asia, for example, the Chinese combine Buddhism with Ancestor worship.

It is noteworthy that native religions have persisted among indigenous peoples in the face of foreign religions (e.g., Christianity). The locals seem to connect their self or group identity to native religions. In other words, native religions enable a "native self," whereas foreign religions produce an "acquired self." When both native and foreign religions are embraced, the "native self" is made to co-exist with the "acquired self."

Cross-cultural psychologist, John Berry (1997), explicates four outcomes in his acculturation model. Berry's (1997) model, although intended for immigrants in a new culture, has implications on how a foreign religion could have an impact on indigenous people. The acculturation outcomes include:

- Assimilation: This occurs when a person of an indigenous culture adopts the norms and practices of a foreign culture (or religion).

- Integration: This happens when a person is accepting of both indigenous and foreign cultures (or religions) at the same time.
- Separation: This occurs when a person rejects a foreign culture (or religion) and keeps his or her indigenous culture (or religion).
- Marginalization. This happens when a person rejects his or her own indigenous culture (or religion) and also a foreign culture (or religion).

In Berry's model (1997), a separation behavior would reflect the "native self," whereas an assimilation behavior would be synonymous to the "acquired self." While Separation seems to be the opposite of Assimilation, accommodation behavior would be an integration of both. A person's choice of an acculturation strategy might be influenced by the following factors:

1. Assimilation: Historically, foreign missionaries have played important roles in indigenous peoples' decision to embrace a foreign religion. Foreign missionaries share the tenets of their faith but also meet the needs of the locals (e.g. medical or educational). When pertinent or basic needs are being met alongside the proselytization of a faith, it becomes easier to assimilate a foreign religion. This strategy has been successful in non-Western/developing societies.
2. Separation: As described earlier, practices of local religion help to define a native self, whereas a foreign religion defines an acquired self. To embrace a foreign religion is to lose the native self.
3. Integration: This is a compromise of both "native" and "acquired" selves. When appropriate both identities are used accordingly, similar to individuals displaying more than one identity in the workplace as a professional and at home as a parent.

Impacts of Individualism and Collectivism

Generally, in Western/developed countries and in non-Western /developing societies people have belief systems and practices that influence death, dying and bereavement differently. Westerners are largely individualistic, whereas non-Westerners are mostly collectivistic. Whites make up the dominant group in the United States and

Canada, and the cultures of both countries are largely individualistic, thereby impacting on end-of-life decisions that reflect individualistic values. Between 1998-2017 in the US, 4,249 prescriptions were issued for physician-assisted suicide (PAS) patients. Of the 66.3% patients who used the drugs to end their lives, 94.2% were White (euthanasia.procon.org, 2019). In Figure 10.1, besides Colombia, countries from around the world are listed that approve of physician-assisted suicide or euthanasia, and these are predominantly Western nations with individualistic tendencies.

Traditional/Cultural Practices

Most times, religious practices and traditional/cultural practices are aligned, because religion serves as guidepost for cultural values, beliefs and practices (e.g., in Middle Eastern countries where Islam is

Figure 10.1
Countries where Physician-Assisted Suicide or Euthanasia is Legal

Country	Physician-Assisted Suicide	Euthanasia
Belgium	X	X
Canada	X	
Colombia		X
Finland	X	
Germany	X	
Luxembourg	X	X
Netherlands	X	X
Switzerland	X	
USA: 8 states and the District of Columbia	X	

Source: Euthanasia.procon.org, July 20, 2016; https://euthanasia.procon.org/euthanasia-physician-assisted-suicide-around-the-sorld/

the dominant religion). However, some cultural practices may evolve independent of religion, from learning giving rise to superstitions. For example, in Estonia where "highly religious" adults make up only 7% of the population, superstitious belief about death and dying is prevalent, especially in the rural areas. Estonians believe that opening doors and windows speed up the escape of the deceased's spirit during funerals (e.g., Estonica.org, n.d.). In parts of Europe a belief is that mirrors in a dead person's house should be covered, because if you saw yourself in a mirror you could join the dead person shortly thereafter.

Influence of Modernization on Traditional Values

In New Zealand, a *funeral celebrant* is used to officiate in burial ceremonies instead of a priest (e.g., Schwass, 2005). The funeral celebrant legitimizes and celebrates the secular lifestyle of the deceased (e.g., Schafer, 2011), unlike a priest who is less likely to do so. Also, locations for funerals have shifted away from the church to include community and school halls, sports clubs, outdoors, or homes of family/ friends of the deceased (e.g. Raudon, 2011). In addition, to enable friends and relatives in distant locations to participate, funerals are livestreamed.

Reciprocal Influence of Traditional Values on Modernization

Traditional values impact on modernity, as well. For example, in New Zealand the Maori's traditional belief of taking a dead body home to keep it 'warm," as opposed to leaving it at a mortuary in a "cold" state, is embraced across ethnic groups. After experiencing modernization, people are likely to revert to traditional ways of doing things if it is to their benefit. In Brazil, also, bereaved persons seek Spiritism for explanation on cause of the death of a loved one, when Christian explanations prove unsatisfactory. The movement in practices is not always from tradition to modernity but from modernity to tradition, also.

Accommodation Behavior (Combining non-Western and Western Beliefs and Values)

In South America where the dominant religion is Christianity, members of minority ethnic groups combine Christian practices with traditional religions in death, dying and bereavement beliefs. In North America where the widely practiced religion is Christianity, many Christians also believe in "evil eye" as a cause of death. However, when Christian practices are akin to traditional religious practices, cognitive dissonance is reduced. For example, among Afro-Surinamese, some burial practices satisfy both Christian and traditional religions (e.g., van der Pijl, 2016). For example, prior to the wake (referred to as *dede oso*), a table is set with a white tablecloth, a glass of water and a lit white candle. In Christianity, the water symbolizes purification and the lit candle hope and resurrection in Christ. However, in traditional religion these items help to connect the living with the dead. Also, in Christianity the color white represents purity and affinity with Christ, but in traditional religion it is the dress code that strengthens a connection with ancestors during the period of intense mourning. Such symbolism that aligns Christianity and traditional religion help to strengthen accommodation behavior.

Worden's (2008) Four tasks of mourning suggests the following for a bereaved person: 1) accept the reality of the loss, e.g., attend the funeral, 2) feel the pain of the loss (e.g., cry), 3) replace the deceased's roles or responsibilities, e.g., become a breadwinner, and 4) memorialize the deceased and move on with life, e.g., form new relationships. To memorialize the deceased and move on with one's life, however, it is important to know the cause of death, especially among non-Westerners. Besides Western medical autopsy reports, seeking a "spiritual" autopsy report from spiritual healers is important due to accommodation behavior. It is also important if the individual has adopted a *separatist* acculturation strategy (e.g., Berry 1997). In Brazil, Regina Bousso and colleagues (2011) report that neither Catholicism nor Protestantism provided answers to the cause of loss, so the bereaved had to seek further explanations in Spiritism. Not resolving the issue surrounding the cause of death can delay the move to memorialize the deceased and move on with life. Among Afro-Surinamese, the deceased must be given a "proper burial" based on tradition and customs. Otherwise, the deceased will not be happy and will make life difficult for the living. Without a proper burial and/or if the deceased is unhappy, memorializing the deceased and moving on with life might become difficult.

MOTIVATIONAL BASIS FOR A DECEASED-FOCUSED
APPROACH TO BEREAVEMENT

Dennis Klass et al. (1996) suggest that bereaved individuals maintain *continuing bond* with deceased loved ones (supposedly after making practical adjustments to move on with life) through letter writing, talking to the deceased, visiting where the deceased is buried, or feeling the presence of the deceased. Just like in Worden's model, the bereaved person is the focus of attention and does what she or he wants to feel wholesome or healed. The *deceased-focused approach* to bereavement proposes an alternative model instead. The deceased person is the focus of attention and not the bereaved, who now represents the deceased who is no longer living. The bereaved should do what would be pleasing to the deceased and receive both satisfaction and healing in return. Earlier examples point to the bereaved trying to please the deceased, which include providing a "proper" burial according to tradition and norms and including in the decedent's coffin the deceased's favorite items such as cigarettes, food or drinks (e.g., among the Estonians). After burial, also, attempt at pleasing the deceased continues with statements as: "This funeral is a celebration of John's life because he wouldn't want us to be sad."

With such a statement, the bereaved is demonstrating a willingness to be a *surrogate* of the deceased who no longer exists. In grief recovery, therefore, the bereaved needs to adjust to his or her loss (which most grief models advocate) *but* also needs to adjust for the deceased's loss as well. This dual adjustment to grief could help in bringing about healing and satisfaction. In Ancestor worship (and in folk belief among secular people, also) the deceased is believed to be aware of happenings in the world of the living, and the deceased would be pleased to know that adjustments are being made on their behalf. For example, the US economy lost 40 million jobs due from the COVID-19 pandemic in the early months of 2020. Following the job loss, an unexpected gain of 2.5 million jobs was announced by the Bureau of Labor Statistics on May 5, 2020. With that excitement, President Trump said it was a great day for the country *and* for George Floyd whose death from police brutality had sparked nationwide and international protests that were ongoing. According to Nicholas Wu (2020), President Trump said George Floyd was "hopefully looking down and feeling good" because of the jobs report (https://www.usa today.com/story/news/politics/2020/06/05/trump-economy-event -george-floyd-hopefully-looking-down/3154495001/). From his statement, President Trump felt that late George Floyd would be pleased with actions taken about the unemployment situation in the country. In return, president might have had a feeling of satisfaction and healing. There is no indication, however, that President Trump had a prior relationship or knowledge at a personal level of George Floyd before his death, to know what would be pleasing to George Floyd. However, of worthy note is that the president made the deceased the focus of his attention, in receiving satisfaction and healing from the loss. In the deceased-focused approach, perspective-taking (cf.: Robert Selman's Perspective-taking theory 1980) is an important element.

Intrinsic Versus Extrinsic Motivation

The motivation for a deceased-focused approach to grief may be intrinsic or extrinsic. In intrinsic motivation the bereaved person receives gratification in doing things she or he perceives as pleasing to the deceased, without expecting anything in return or in trying to avoid punishment for failure of doing such by the deceased. In extrinsic motivation, however, the opposite is the case: The bereaved person's actions are based on perceived gains or punishments in doing what is pleasing to the deceased. In Ancestor worship, for example, the bereaved person's actions are motivated by the perceived goodwill or blessings to be derived, or the punishment to be avoided in pleasing the dead. As stated earlier, the deceased-focused approach is predicated on Robert Selman's perspective-taking theory (1980), whereby people are able to demonstrate the ability to understand the feelings and perspectives of others; and in this case, the decedent's. In the deceased-focused approach, doing what is pleasing to the deceased should be based on intrinsic motivation (as opposed to extrinsic motivation), because intrinsic motivation would lead to optimal development and psychological wellness (e.g., Ryan & Deci, 2017).

Key Terms

Acculturation model
Acquired self
Deceased-focused approach

Native self
Physician-assisted suicide
Religion
Surrogate
Traditional cultural practices

SUMMARY

The following factors can help to enrich existing death, dying and bereavement models:

1. Influence of religion
2. Impact of individualism and collectivism
3. Traditional /cultural practices
4. Influence of modernization on traditional values
5. Reciprocal influence of traditional values on modernization
6. Accommodation behavior (accepting both non-Western and (Western values)

As an alternative, the deceased-focused approach to bereavement is predicated on Robert Selman's perspective-taking theory (1980), whereby people are able to demonstrate the ability to understand the feelings and perspective of others, and in this case, that of the deceased. To experience growth and wholeness, intrinsic motivation as opposed to extrinsic motivation is required.

Review Questions

1. What contributions can be made to Worden's four tasks of mourning?
2. What contributions can be made to the Continuing Bond model of mourning?
3. What is the difference between a native self and an acquired self? How would you describe yourself?
4. What strategies are available in acquiring a foreign culture or religion to an individual?
5. How does modernity impact on traditional practices and vice-versa? Have you or are you aware of someone who reverted to traditional ways of doing things from modern ways? Why?

Additional Readings

Parkes, C. M., Laungani, P., & Young, W. (Eds.). (2015). *Death and bereavement across cultures.* New York: Routledge.

Selin, H., & Rakoff, R. N. (Eds.). (2019). *Death across cultures: Death and dying in non-Western cultures.* New York: Springer.

Chapter 11

HELP FOR THE DYING AROUND THE WORLD

Chapter Outline

Learning objectives
Factors influencing types of help
Influence of Individualism on types of help
Physician-assisted suicide
Euthanasia
Living will
Death Doula
Dying2learn: online course for developing end-of-life competencies
Native patient navigator for ethnic minorities
Death tourism
Palliative care
Beliefs in the supernatural
Complementary and alternative medicine (CAM)
Traditional medicine
The dying person's choice of spending the remainder time on earth
Summary
Key terms
Review questions
Additional readings

Learning Objectives

LO1: Understand the role of individualism in providing help for dying persons

LO2: Explain the role of death doulas in providing help for dying persons

LO3: Understand the Native Patient Navigator's role in navigating services for dying persons

LO4: Describe types of palliative care within healthcare systems

LO5: Understand types of palliative care outside of healthcare systems

LO6: Explain factors likely to influence how dying persons spend their remainder days on earth

LO7: Explain how educational programs help to prepare people for the experience of dying

FACTORS INFLUENCING TYPES OF HELP

The type of help available to dying persons across the world would be influenced by cultural values, individual beliefs and available resources. As earlier discussed, the Western/developed societies place high importance on individualism, empowering individuals to make decisions based on personal values and beliefs, as opposed to decisions made on behalf of the individual by others. A dying person is not treated differently.

The following are examples of practices that reflect on individualism and enables a dying person to maintain a sense of personal control.

Physician-Assisted Suicide

In physician-assisted suicide, a dying person approaches a physician to prescribe a lethal dose of medication that he/she would take to terminate life. If living is considered unbearable, the terminal patient makes a choice to die rather than to live. In the USA physician-assisted suicide is legal in eight states and in the District of Columbia. It is also legal in several Western countries, including Australia (in Victoria), Belgium, Canada, the Netherlands, Luxembourg, and Switzerland. Generally, the laws require that the dying patient is given six months or less to live, is expected to be of a sound mind, and must make more than one request for this option to be granted (e.g., Emanuel, Onwuteaka-Phiipsen, Urwin, & Cohen, 2016). The advocates of physician-assisted suicide, among other reasons, point to the dying person's need for autonomy and personal liberty. In 2019 in the US state of Oregon, the residents who took advantage of that state's Death with Dignity Act identified the following primary reasons which appeared to reflect on individualistic values: decreased inability to participate in enjoyable activities (90%), loss of autonomy (87%), and loss of dignity (72%) (e.g., Oregon Health Authority; March 6, 2020; https://www.oregon.gov/oha/ph/providerpartnerresources/evaluationresearch/deathwithdignityact/pages/ar-index.aspx). In Colombia in South America where physician-assisted suicide is also legal, Whites and mestizos (a mixed race of White European and Amerindian ancestries) make up the largest population (87.6%) (https://www.cia.gov/library/publications/the-world-factbook/geos/co.html). Given the predominant makeup of the population, Western individualistic tendencies are expectedly valued, as well.

Euthanasia

With Euthanasia, a dying patient gives a physician permission to take direct action that would end his or her life. Euthanasia is not practiced in the US, but is legal in Switzerland, Canada, Belgium, the Netherlands and Luxembourg. The guidelines for euthanasia are similar to physician-assisted suicide: the patient must be of a sound mind, the request is made more than once and the patient must be terminally ill with six months or less to live. However, euthanasia and physician-assisted suicide are different. In physician-assisted suicide, the patient may not follow through in taking the lethal medication prescribed by the physician. In the US state of Oregon, of the 290 people who received a physician's prescription for a lethal dose of medication in 2019, only 188 ingested it to end their lives (Oregon Health Authority; 2020, March 6). Some of the patients might have had a rethink of their initial planned action—the type of flexibility not accorded by euthanasia. Also, the dying person might have been subjected to external influences or pressure, including from family, friends, clergy or loved ones, to not follow through with ingesting the prescribed lethal medication. In this respect, euthanasia has an advantage over physician-assisted suicide in actualizing individualistic values.

Living Will

As a legal document, a living will provides an "advance directive" on the type of medical treatment and care a person wishes to have when not able to make a decision at a future time. It places choice-making on no other person but the dying person, who may also wish to delegate the decision to a medical power of attorney or a health-care surrogate in the future. Most US states require that a living will form be signed and notarized with at least one witness (in some states two witnesses) (e.g., Eforms, n.d.; https://eforms.com/living-will/).

Death Doula

A *doula* is a Greek term for "a woman who provides social, emotional and practical support to other women during pregnancy, birth and the postnatal period. She is not a health professional and does not provide any clinical care" (Spiby, McLeish, Green, & Darwin, 2016, p. 1). The emergence of doulas in the death and dying industry is borne out of a similar need to have someone provide social, emotional, and practical support for the dying person, also. The type of support is non-specific but based on the dying person's needs. Death doulas help to fill gaps created by the paucity of healthcare professionals at the end of life (e.g., Rawlings, Lister, Miller-Lewis, Tieman, & Swetenham, 2020). They also pick up where the healthcare provider's role drops. Generally, the role of a death doula could be summed up as "holding a compassionate space" (Elliott, 2011, p. 29).

Researcher Amanda Phelan and colleagues (2018) studied 458 community nurses in Ireland and they reported on the "missed care" delivery that persons in need of medical help, including the dying, experienced. With more families that are geographically dispersed and more women in the workforce, death doulas provide a much-needed service in the absence of family members or loved ones. In Europe, up to 40% of family caregivers are in paid employment (e.g., Christensen et al., 2009), and in the US and Canada and Japan the absence of family caregivers is gaining more prominence (e.g., Hilbrecht et al., 2017; Ireson et al., 2018). Though death doulas have been criticized for not coming under strict oversight, their role is to meet the personal needs of the dying person, which makes an oversight uncalled for, just as a family member in providing care to a dying loved one is not subject to oversight regulation (e.g., Rawlings et al., 2020).

The services of death doulas are provided independently of or through established systems such as hospice or hospitals, as paid or voluntary basis. In reviewing reports on the roles of death doulas, Deb Rawlings and colleagues (2020) likened their roles to those of a "senior daughter" in the family, but death doulas do not have to be gender specific.

The International End of Life Doula Association (INELDA), an organization founded in February 2015 to foster training and using of death doulas in hospices, hospital and communities notes the roles of doulas as providing ". . . emotional, spiritual, and physical support at an intensely personal and crucial time. They assist the dying people in finding meaning, in creating legacy projects, and in planning for how their last days will unfold. Doulas also guide and support loved ones through the last days of life, easing the suffering of grief in its early stages" (https://www.linkedin.com/company/international-end-of-life-doula-association-inedla-).The University of Vermont, in collaboration with Cabot Cooperative Farms, offers an 8-week online certificate program in death doula, with the following Learning Objectives that empowers the dying person:

- Become prepared to work in harmony with a client's chosen care team (potentially) including community members, family, friends, and medical practitioners to fill-in support gaps as needed and heighten a client's feelings of empowerment and self-efficacy.
- Respect appropriate professional/personal boundaries while keeping the client's best interest in mind at all times.
- Understand common terminal conditions and diseases (and their associated symptoms and progressive courses of decline), pain management practices, the active dying process, and helpful interventions to ease suffering.
- Describe the role and scope of an End-Of-Life Doula and apply the core skills of providing unconditional positive regard and nonjudgmental support while comfortably holding space, companioning, and engaging in open, accepting dialog with clients.
- Garner a wide variety of details about special populations based on religious beliefs and cultural norms, as well as the unique challenges associated with pediatric death and end-stage dementia.
- Recognize and support the stages and facets of anticipatory grief, mourning, and bereavement.
- Effectively refer patients and families to other local professionals, organizations, support groups, and businesses that provide offerings to those at the end of life.

- Engage in meaningful conversations with clients and assist with legacy projects to encourage emotional acceptance and peaceful preparation.
- Develop seemingly endless, practical methods of decreasing anxiety/suffering by utilizing visualizations, guided imagery, simple massage techniques, as well as creating a comforting energetic space for clients which feels calming and relaxing.
- Support clients in developing vigil wishes and values-based advance directives.
- Nurture a protective, calm presence and environment during vigil sitting.
- Offer acute bereavement support and appropriate referrals to a client's family and friends after death. (https://learn.uvm.edu/program/end-of-life-doula-at-uvm/end-of-life-doula-certificate/).

Dying2Learn: Online Course for Developing End-of-life Competencies

In addition to death doulas, other programs help in filling in for the shortage of medical care providers by developing competencies in people on handling end-of-life situations for either self or others. In Australia, through an online course some researchers have explored whether exposing people to death discussions would improve on their death competency (e.g., Miller-Lewis et al., 2020). Using the Massive Open Online Course (MOOC) at Flinders University a *Dying2Learn* program was designed to engage community members in discussions about death and dying and how to foster care for the dying. One hundred and thirty-four participants completed a Coping-With-Death scale, both before and after the course. Death competence was measured based on the range of attitudes and capabilities people indicated in dealing with death. After taking the course, participants showed significant improvements, especially those who completed more of the course. A course such as this might empower individuals to prepare for their own dying experience as well as equip them for taking care of the dying.

NATIVE PATIENT NAVIGATOR FOR ETHNIC MINORITIES

In ethnic minority communities experiencing health disparities, a Native Patient Navigator system has been utilized as a support structure for people requiring help in navigating the healthcare system, including the terminally ill. Based on cultural competence, the Native Patient Navigator is able to advocate for and attend to the dying person's needs and also enjoys the trust of the dying person. Among the Latinos, palliative care outcomes for patients with advanced cancer was improved using the native patient navigation. In a study of 223 patients (randomly assigned into two groups), patients who had the benefit of native patient navigators were more likely to discuss advance care planning with family members and providers and also indicated they would recommend hospice for themselves or others, when compared to their counterparts who did not have the same opportunity (e.g., Fischer, Min, Kline & Fink, 2017). The native patient navigator concept has been successfully applied to Native American Indians, also, resulting in good healthcare outcomes (e.g., Burhansstipanov et al., 2014). The native patient navigators are trained to ensure they are equipped to operate on behalf of their clients based on professional standards (e.g., Rocque et al., 2017). If programs designed to help dying people, especially ethnic minority group members who are economically disadvantaged, are not offered on a voluntary basis, they may be cost prohibitive because families facing end-of-life experience are already burdened with financial expenses (e.g., Rowland, Hanratty, Pilling, van den Berg, & Grande, 2017).

DEATH TOURISM

As earlier noted, physician-assisted suicide or euthanasia is not legal in every country. Therefore, *death tourism* involves moving from a location with no assistance for the dying to a place where such is provided. For example, in the US, physician-assisted suicide is legal in only eight states and Washington DC. In 2014, Brittany Maynard was diagnosed with a form of brain cancer with a prognosis of six months to live. She lived in California where physician-assisted suicide was not legal and moved to Oregon State to take advantage of the Oregon's Death with Dignity law (Maynard, 2014: https://www.cnn.com /2014/10/07/opinion/maynard-assisted-suicide-cancer-dignity).

PALLIATIVE CARE

A significant part to providing help to the dying is making palliative care available to those who need it. Palliative care includes helping the terminally ill patient whose situation is incurable, by preventing and treating symptoms including pain, insomnia, shortness of breath or lack of appetite relating to the illness. Palliative care also includes taking care of the emotional, social, practical, and spiritual issues that accompany an illness. In palliative care, the goal is to make the dying person feel better in a holistic way. Palliative care may benefit a terminal patient with a disease such as cancer, heart disease, lung diseases, kidney diseases, Alzheimer's disease or HIV/AIDS. Usually, it is provided within a healthcare system, with care providers including doctors, nurses, registered dietitians, social workers, psychologists, massage therapists and chaplains. In the USA, Crossroads Hospice and Palliative Care (2017), for example, keeps its patients comfortable using the following opioid regime as painkillers in managing pain symptoms:

- Morphine (Roxanol, MS Contin)
- Oxycodone (Oxycontin)
- Methadone (Dolophine)
- Hydromorphone (Dilaudid)
  (https://www.crossroadshospice.com/hospice-palliative-care-blog/2017/september/07/all-you-need-to-know-about-pain-management-in-hospice/).

The Economist Intelligence Unit in 2015 conducted a study that ranked 80 countries on Quality of Death based on palliative care provided. They used the following dimensions as measures of palliative care: 1) palliative and healthcare environment, 2) human resources, 3) affordability, 4) quality of care, and 5) community engagement. Based on interviews conducted with local palliative care experts in the respective societies, they ranked the countries as shown in Table 11.1.

Besides Taiwan, countries in the top 10 (in asterisk) are Western nations: Australia, Belgium, France, Germany, Ireland, the Netherlands, New Zealand, UK and USA. With death tourism, however, a dying person can seek palliative care wherever it is offered. For example, around the world Buddhist centers offer to help the dying who

Table 11.1
Palliative Care Ranking of Countries with the Top 10 in Asterisk, 2015

Country in alphabetical order	Palliative care ranking; rank/80
Argentina	32
*Australia	2
Austria	17
Bangladesh	79
*Belgium	5
Botswana	72
Brazil	42
Bulgaria	62
Canada	11
Chile	27
China	71
Colombia	68
Costa Rica	29
Cuba	36
Czech Republic	33
Denmark	19
Dominican Republic	75
Ecuador	40
Egypt	56
Ethiopia	70
Finland	20
*France	10

continued

Table 11.1—*Continued*

Country in alphabetical order	Palliative care ranking; rank/80
*Germany	7
Ghana	51
Greece	56
Guatemala	74
Hong Kong	22
Hungary	41
India	67
Indonesia	53
Iran	73
Iraq	80
*Ireland	4
Israel	25
Italy	21
Japan	14
Jordan	37
Kazakhstan	50
Kenya	63
Lithuania	30
Malawi	66
Malaysia	38
Mexico	43
Mongolia	28

continued

Table 11.1—*Continued*

Country in alphabetical order	Palliative care ranking; rank/80
Morocco	52
Myanmar	76
*Netherlands	8
*New Zealand	3
Nigeria	77
Norway	13
Panama	31
Peru	49
Philippines	78
Poland	26
Portugal	24
Puerto Rico	46
Romania	64
Russia	48
Saudi Arabia	60
Singapore	12
Slovakia	55
South Africa	34
South Korea	18
Spain	23
Sri Lanka	65
Sweden	16

continued

Table 11.1—*Continued*

Country in alphabetical order	Palliative care ranking; rank/80
Switzerland	15
*Taiwan	6
Tanzania	54
Thailand	44
Turkey	47
Uganda	35
*UK	1
Ukraine	69
*US	9
Uruguay	39
Venezuela	45
Vietnam	58
Zambia	61
Zimbabwe	59

Source: The Economist Intelligence Unit, 2015;
https://eiuperspectives.economist.com/sites/default/files/images/2015%20Quality%20of%20
Death%20Index%20Country%20Profiles_Oct%206%20FINAL.pdf).

seek to be at peace with death. The organization, *Rigba,* teaches seminars on death and dying based on Tibetian Buddhism. It has locations around the US, including Boston, New York, San Diego, San Francisco, Seattle, and Washington, DC. Rigba also has locations in France, Ireland and Germany. Rigba's founder, Sogyal Rinpoche, is the author of *The Tibetian Book of Living and Dying* (e.g., Rigba, n.d.; https://www.rigpa.org/).

BELIEFS IN THE SUPERNATURAL

In non-Western societies, the belief in the supernatural as a means of palliative care is commonplace. In Western societies such a belief is present, as well. Researchers suggest that the predisposition to believe in the supernatural is biologically wired because people have a need to find meaning to or ascribe reason to uncertain situations (e.g., Norenzayan et al., 2006). However, to bring this pre-disposition to fruition, learning is important in terms of what and whom to believe (or not to believe). Around the world religious, spiritual and meditational practices are pervasive influences. They help to accentuate the predisposition to belief, including in pain management. To understand palliative care as only occurring within the healthcare system may fail to capture the importance of beliefs in the supernatural for the terminally ill. For example, from clinical research and reports religious people are less likely to experience anxiety and depression (e.g., Plante, 2010). To some religious people, pain is interpreted as their "cross" to bear. In Hinduism and Buddhism, pain might be explained as a consequence of a previous action, whereas to the Muslim it must be the will of Allah—with believers less likely to seek palliative care within the healthcare system (e.g., Dedeli & Kaptan, 2013). Around the world, in 2015, the Muslim faith had 1.8 billion followers (Lipkar, 2017; Pew Research Center; https://www.pewresearch.org/fact-tank /2017/08/09/muslims-and-islam-key-findings-in-the-u-s-and-around-the -world/), and they are mostly in Central Asia, Indonesia, the Middle East, and North and Sub-Saharan Africa (e.g., Pew Research Center, 2013; https://assets.pewresearch.org/wp-content/uploads/sites/11 /2013/04/worlds-muslims-religion-politics-society-full-report.pdf). It is noteworthy that on the Economist Intelligence Unit's global ranking in palliative care, Indonesia, with the largest Muslim population in the world, ranked fifty-third (e.g., Pew Research, Center 2010a: https: //www.pewforum.org/2010/11/04/muslim-population-of-indonesia/). Also, India ranked at sixty-seventh and 80% of its population is made up of Hindus (Pew Research Center, 2012: https://www.pewforum.org /2012/12/18/global-religious-landscape-hindu/).

Some studies have been able to demonstrate the impact of spirituality and religious beliefs on pain and fatigue. A study of 37,000 participants, ages 51 and older, report that participants with religious and spiritual backgrounds do cope better with pain and chronic fatigue than those without (e.g., Baetz & Bowen, 2008). Both spirituality and religious beliefs helped in providing meaning to life and death (Cusick, 2003). Also, prayers and support from fellow believers help to provide relief from pain (e.g., Unruh, 2007). Prayer has been reported to improve the mood of people experiencing pain (e.g., Smith, McCullough & Poll, 2003).

Researcher Katja Wiech and colleagues (2008) used Functional Magnetic Resonance Imaging (fMRI) in identifying areas of the brain responsible for modulating pain intensity. Two groups (12 practicing Catholics and 12 non-religious/non-spiritual individuals) participated in their study. The practicing Catholics were shown a picture of the Virgin Mary, while the non-religious/non-spiritual group saw the picture of an unknown woman. Although both groups were equally sensitive to pain, the practicing Catholics experienced less pain than the non-religious/non-spiritual group. The Catholic group reported being in a calm, meditative mood when presented with the photo of the Virgin Mary. Thus, the contemplation (either visually or meditatively) of a powerful religious figure could help with relief of pain for a religious dying patient in distress. The part of the brain activated for the Catholics (and not the non-religious/non-spiritual group) was the right ventrolateral pre-frontal cortex (VLPFC), a region that helps to reinterpret a stimulus to minimize its emotional impact, including negative emotions (e.g., Goldin, McRae, Ramel, & Gross, 2008; McRae et al., 2010).

COMPLEMENTARY AND ALTERNATIVE MEDICINE (CAM)

Besides spirituality and religious beliefs, complementary and alternative medicine (CAM) has been used to provide palliative care for the dying. Across the world, CAM is used for both health prevention and symptom relief. *Complementary medicine* is used to augment Western conventional medicine, whereas *Alternative medicine* is used as a replacement to Western medicine (e.g., National Cancer Institute, n.d.; Complementary and alternative medicine; http://www.cancer .gov/cancertopics/cam). Most times, people resort to CAM when conventional Western medicine fails to provide symptom relief (e.g., Zeng, Wang, Ward & Hume, 2018). In Europe herbal medicine, homeopathy, chiropractic, acupuncture and reflexology are most frequently used as CAM. They are mostly used for relief of back problems, depression, insomnia, severe headaches or migraines and stomach or intestinal problems (e.g., Frass, Strassl, Friehs et al., 2012). According to Ralph Muecke and colleagues (2016), in Germany 40% of cancer patients use CAM at some point during or after therapy. CAM use is common among women (60-90%) with breast cancer and gynecological problems (e.g., Molassiotis, Fernadez-Ortega, Pud et al., 2006). Interactions have been noted, however, in patients who combine conventional Western medicine with CAM (e.g., Zeller, Muenstedt, Stoll et al., 2013). This has led to the use of CAM as *alternative* medicine only, especially in advanced cancer patients (e.g., Micke, Bruns, Glatzel et al., 2009).

TRADITIONAL MEDICINE

Traditional medicine could be used as either complementary medicine or alternative medicine. In reviewing traditional medical practices across different cultures of the world, researcher Ann Lichtenstein and colleagues (2017) conclude that traditional medical practices are an admixture of the cultural, social, psychological and spiritual elements of a people, with the outcome being healing for the infirm. Unlike Western medicine, the knowledge and practice of traditional medicine is generally not conveyed through formal educational settings but passed down as oral tradition through generations. In traditional medicine there is a strong belief in the supernatural. Imbalance in the physical (body), psychological (mind) and spiritual (supernatural) realms is believed to cause pain, suffering and disease. Therefore, the practice of traditional medicine is to bring about a balance to these three aspects. Traditional medicine serves as a form of holistic medical practice. In India, *Ayurveda,* which means knowledge of life and longevity, is a form of traditional medicine (e.g., Dwarakanath, 1970; National Cancer Institute, n.d.; Complementary and alternative medicine; http://www.cancer.gov/cancertopics/cam.). In Ayurveda, the suppression of natural impulses is said to result in ill health. For example, to hold up the urge to sneeze could result in bodily pain (e.g., Pathak, Raut & Vaidya, 2008). In addition, moderation is emphasized in all one does (e.g., Wujastyk, 2003). Among Native American Indians healing comes from sweating because they believe that sweating purifies the body, mind and soul. Thus, people in need of healing participate in sweating ceremonies (e.g., Garrett et al.,

2011). In Africa, witchcraft or sorcery is believed to cause illness and with appeasement of ancestral spirits comes healing (e.g., Essien, 2013).

In Mexico and Latin America, *Curanderismo* (belief in folk healing) is common practice. The origin of disease is said to be supernatural, and healing is sought from a priest (curandero) who is believed to be spiritually chosen and has supernatural abilities to heal and cure illnesses (e.g., Padilla et al., 2001). Traditional Chinese medicine uses herbs for treatment which are boiled and mixed with honey for oral application. Sometimes the herbs are burned and used in combination with acupuncture. The burned herbs produce heat and when applied close to the body, energy is distributed—a process called *moxibustion* (e.g., Dong & Zhang, 2001).

From reviewing traditional medical practices across cultures, Ann Lichtenstein and colleagues (2017) describe the use of herbs as common in healing practices. In non-Western developing countries, the use of traditional medicine may be fostered by a) a lack of access to Western medical facilities (e.g., hospitals} and/or b) a belief in traditional medicine's efficacy. In resource-poor societies acute illnesses are common (e.g., infectious diseases), and due to a lack of adequate Western medical facilities and practitioners to diagnosis cases of terminal illness, death occurs unexpectedly. Therefore, within available health care systems palliative care is rudimentary or nonexistent.

THE DYING PERSON'S CHOICE OF SPENDING THE REMAINDER TIME ON EARTH

Spending the remainder time on earth is an important aspect to providing help to the dying person, because his or her time on earth is closing out and certain actions need to be taken. The following factors, however, can influence how dying persons are likely to spend their remainder time on earth:

- Has the dying person accepted that death is imminent? If not, it is likely that the search for a cure would occupy their remainder time on earth. In the US, studies show that most African Americans die in the hospital because of a desire to seek for a cure. For example, researcher Nan Tracy Zheng and colleagues (2011) report on racial disparities in in-hospital death and hospice use at the end of life among 49,048 long-term care residents in 555 New York state nursing homes. When compared to Whites (24.07%) almost twice as many Blacks (40.33%) died in the hospital, but when compared to Whites (17.39), fewer Blacks (11.55%) used hospice. Socio-cultural factors might be influential in value differences.

- The health status of the dying person is an important consideration. Even if the dying person accepts that death is imminent, the individual's poor health status could limit the choice of possibilities. For example, if the dying person would like to travel the world, this choice could be made difficult if ambulatory capacity is limited. Researchers have identified challenges that dying persons are likely to face in traveling the world including lack of confidence, loneliness, fitness to travel, medical needs in a foreign country, and immunization (e.g., Willson, McIntosh, Morgan & Saunders, 2018) . The Grove Hotel in Bouremouth, UK offers a 24-hour nursing cover for terminally ill patrons. On its website, it has the following statement: "Welcome to The Grove in Bournemouth, a unique hotel offering a beautiful holiday retreat for cancer patients and those with life threatening illnesses. Carers, families and friends are all welcome" (http://www.thegrovebournemouth.co.uk/; n.d.). With more hotels offering such an opportunity around the world, the terminally ill could embark on "terminal tourism."

- How they wish to be remembered: The remainder days might help the dying person to focus more on how she or he wishes to be remembered or on symbolic immortality, if that had not been addressed previously. The terminal days bring into sharper focus such thoughts than previously contemplated. As mentioned earlier, a death doula can assist with terminal or legacy projects.

- Mending relationships with loved ones and friends and forgiving yourself and others: People might decide to use their remainder days in mending fences, asking for forgiveness from those they believe had been hurt by their actions or deeds. They would like to depart on a good note; perhaps spurred by the need to be remembered in a positive light. Taylor Tagg (2017, December 6; https://www.huffpost.com/entry/the-five-people-to-forgiv_b_9439370) identified the following as "the five people to forgive before you die":

1. Mom and dad: Given their best intentions, they made some mistakes along the way raising you.
2. Siblings (and/or your children): They may be difficult at times and is easy to hold a grudge or resentment against them.
3. Enemy: These are persons who significantly wounded you and include former lovers, abusers, bullies, bosses, etc.
4. Spouse or significant other: Their daily challenge to help you become a better person may sometimes be misplaced and could lead to resentment.
5. Yourself: There could be regrets about those you let down, about your actions, and the goals you fail to accomplish in life. Psychologist Erik Erickson (1958, 1963) called the last stage in his psychosocial developmental process "Integrity versus Despair," suggesting that some people might look back at their life with regrets in guiding their remainder days on earth.

- Taking care of unfinished business such as completing a project. For some people, the remainder days could be devoted to completing an unfinished project that was started before taking ill or that was spurred by the terminal illness itself. For example, in August 2007 Randolph "Randy" Pausch, a professor of computer science, human-computer interaction and design at Carnegie Mellon University in Pittsburgh, Pennsylvania was given six months or less to live. He had pancreatic cancer. Before his death he gave a lecture entitled, "The Last Lecture: Really Achieving Your Childhood Dreams" and co-authored a book called *The Last Lecture,* which became a *New York Times* bestseller (e.g., Nelson, 2008; Plushnick-Masti, 2008).
- Keeping the house in order, e.g., will, living wills, funeral arrangements, burial arrangements, last-minute instructions, etc. The remainder time on earth could be a time for attending to *housekeeping* issues. Although such issues reflect the values and preferences of the dying person (e.g., where s/he wants to be buried, songs to include at funeral, do-not-resuscitate order, etc.), they also are for the benefit of the surviving loved ones, who might disagree on a range of issues after the dying person's demise (e.g., funeral arrangements, estate distribution). Heleigh Bostwick (n.d.) (https://www.legalzoom.com/articles/10-famous-people-who-died-without-a-will), for example, notes the follow-

ing famous people who died without a will and the consequences of their inactions:

1. *Jimi Hendrix* died in 1970, and the battle over his estate continued over 30 years being a musician whose works continued to generate revenue in the future.
2. *Bob Marley* died in 1981; he knew he had cancer 8 months prior to his death. After his death dozens of claimants to his estate reported worth $30 million came forward.
3. Singer *Sonny Bono* (Salvatore Phillip Bono), who later became a politician, died unexpectedly in a skiing accident. His widow Mary Bono wanted the courts to appoint her administrator of his estate; ex-wife Cher asked to be a claimant and a "love" child showed up as well, compounding the situation.
4. *Stieg Larsson*, a Swedish author, died in 2004. Larsson's estate was divided between his father and his brother, according to Swedish law; but his lifelong partner of 32 years, Eva Gabrielsson, received nothing (except the couple's apartment granted her by Stieg's family).
5. *Pablo Picasso* died in 1973 and left behind an estate that included artwork, five homes, cash, gold and bonds. It took 6 years to eventually settle his estate among six heirs, at a cost of $30 million.
6. *Abraham Lincoln,* 16th president of the United States and a lawyer himself, died in 1865 unexpectedly when he was assassinated.

While Bob Marley's case may not be the ideal, when life is terminal and the dying person is able, the opportunity to keep one's house in order could be taken advantage of in the remainder days.

SUMMARY

1. Based on belief systems and resource disparities, the availability of help for dying persons would differ across the world.
2. In Western/developed societies Individualism is pervasive, with emphasis on empowering the individual to making decisions based on his or her personal values and beliefs, including end-

of-life decisions. Practices that help the dying person to maintain personal control include:
- Physician-assisted suicide
- Euthanasia
- Living will
- Death doula

3. Dying persons have also experienced help from the native patient navigator program for ethnic minority group members, death tourism, palliative care, and through beliefs in the supernatural. Others include the use of complementary and alternative medicine (CAM) and traditional medicine.

4. An important help to dying persons is how they spend the remainder time on earth. Factors likely to influence their choice include the following:

   a. Has the dying person accepted that death is imminent? If not, it is likely that the search for a cure would occupy the remainder of their time on earth.

   b. The health status of the dying person: Even if the dying person has accepted that death is imminent, the dying person's poor health status could limit the choice of possibilities, e.g., traveling the world.

   c. How they wish to be remembered: A death doula can assist with projects such as making a video.

   d. Mending relationships with loved ones and friends and forgiving yourself and others. People might decide to use their remainder days in mending fences, asking for forgiveness from those they believe had been hurt by their actions or deeds. They would like to depart on a good note, perhaps spurred by the need to be remembered in a positive light.

   e. Taking care of unfinished business such as completing a project. For some people, the remainder days could be devoted to completing an unfinished project that was started before taking ill or that was spurred by the terminal illness itself.

   f. Keeping the house in order, e.g., will, living will, funeral arrangement, burial arrangement, last-minute instructions, etc.

Key Terms

Beliefs in the supernatural
Complementary and alternative medicine (CAM)
Death doula
Death tourism
Dying2learn
Euthanasia
Living will
Native patient navigator
Palliative care
Physician-assisted suicide
Remainder time on earth
Traditional Medicine

Review Questions

1. How can a terminal patient be helped during the dying process?
2. Can you list your preference of help from 1 being the most important to 5 being the least important?
3. What are the benefits of having a death doula?
4. Would you consider physician-assisted suicide or euthanasia as helping the dying patient?
5. Outside of the healthcare system, what approaches to palliative care are available to the dying patient?
6. How could a terminal patient spend (or be encouraged to spend) their remainder days on earth?
7. What types of palliative care are available to non-Western/developing societies outside of the healthcare system?

Additional Reading

Doukas, D. J., & Reichel, W. (2007). *Planning for uncertainty: Living wills and other advance directives for you and your family.* Baltimore, MD: Johns Hopkins University Press.

Micozzi, M. (2018). *Fundamentals of complementary, alternative, and integrative medicine.* Philadelphia, PA: Saunders.

Chapter 12

COMMONALITIES AND DIFFERENCES IN DEATH, DYING AND BEREAVEMENT AROUND THE WORLD

Chapter Outline

Learning objectives
Defining death
Standard approaches to defining death
Variations to defining death
Causes of death
Funeral and burial practices
Conventional methods
Unconventional methods
Expanding on grief models
Influence of religion
Conflicting belief systems
Other-centered
Summary
Key terms
Review questions
Additional readings

Learning Objectives

LO1: Examine the definition of death
LO2: Understand the limitations of a universal definition of death
LO3: Examine likely factors that are responsible for being "buried alive"
LO4: Understand conventional funeral and burial practices

LO5: Explain unconventional funeral and burial practices
LO6: Understand the need to expand on existing grief models

DEFINING DEATH

The experience of death, dying and bereavement is universal, and commonalities and differences abound around the world. It is noteworthy of understanding how death should be defined because of its finality. The following are examples from around the world that portray scenarios where death was poorly defined, leading to being "buried alive." In all the mentioned cases, the basis for declaring a person as being dead is the absence of vital signs. This approach appears to be inadequate and if not used with caution, the number of "buried alive" persons might increase.

- A man in Peru who underwent a root canal operation and was under sedation was declared dead. At his funeral Watson Franklin Mandujano Doroteo appeared to be breathing on his own, when some relatives noticed his rib cage rising and falling in his casket. A doctor was called who confirmed that he showed vital signs (e.g., Los Andes, 2017, October 25; https://www .losandes.com.ar/article/view?slug=lo-estaban-velando-se-dieron-cuenta-de-que-respiraba-y-lo-llevaron-al-hospital).
- 78-year-old Walter Williams "passed away" in his home in Lexington, Mississippi due to natural causes. However, as workers at a funeral home began to prepare him for embalming they noticed his legs began to move and he was breathing. Doctors felt a mix of medication might have caused his vital signs to be unresponsive, whereas some relatives speculated that his pacemaker might have turned off (Gander, 2014; https://www.independent .co.uk/news/world/americas/walter-williams-dead-us-man-who -woke-up-in-a-body-bag-dies-two-weeks-later-9191156.html).
- In Egypt 2012, Hamdi Hafez al-Nubi, a 28-year-old man, suffered a heart attack at work. The doctor was signing his death certificate when it was noticed that his body was warm and he was still alive (Independent, 2012; https://www.independent .co.uk/news/world/africa/man-declared-dead-wakes-up-at-his -funeral-in-egypt-7742041.html).

- In the Philippines in 2012, during preparations for her funeral, a 3-year-old awoke in her coffin. The girl's parents' neighbor removed the lid to the coffin to arrange the toddler's body and noticed her head move. She had been declared dead at a local hospital due to a lack of vital signs (Dearden, 2014; https://www .independent.co.uk/news/world/asia/dead-three-year-old-girl -wakes-up-in-coffin-at-her-own-funeral-in-philippines-9604875 .html).
- In Venezuela in 2007, Carlos Camejo, 33 years old, was involved in a highway accident and was declared dead. During autopsy, examiners noticed he was bleeding and quickly stitched him back up. Carlos woke up in the mortuary after experiencing excruciating pain from the incision on his face, as he recalled. Carlos' grieving wife arrived at the mortuary to identify him but instead found her husband in the corridor alive (Reuters, 2007; https://www.reuters.com/article/us-autopsy /dead-man-wakes-up-under-autopsy-knife-idUSN1499758200 70917).
- In South Africa, an ambulance crew picked up a woman from an accident scene with no pulse or breath. She was declared dead and taken to the mortuary. Several hours later someone noticed she was breathing (de Greef, 2018; https://www .nytimes.com/2018/07/02/world/africa/south-africa-wrongly -declared-dead.html).

Standard Approaches to Defining Death

Over the years the definition for death has changed with new criteria, based on the discovery of new technology. Three criteria have been used to define death:

1. *Somatic:* This is a visual inspection of the body without knowing details of the state of internal organs, e.g., decomposition of the body, decapitation or rigor mortis (stiffening of joints and muscles a few hours after death).
2. *Circulatory:* This is an irreversible cessation of circulatory and respiratory functions. A cardiopulmonary test on pulse or heartbeat and of breath is the basis for making conclusions about death. This approach examines 'vital signs." With technological

advancement, however, this approach has become questionable, as heart and lung functions can now be performed artificially.

3. *Neurological:* This is a brain test using an EEG, or electroencephalogram, to determine death. There are two aspects of brain death: death of the whole brain and death of part of the brain or higher brain (cerebral hemispheres) that controls for memory, consciousness, beliefs, and desires. Arguments in favor of the higher brain suggest that this part of the brain controls for what makes us human—absence of which we lose our human essence. The counterargument, however, is that whole brain death includes higher brain death, which helps to avoid possible legal tangles (e.g., Madoff, 2011).

The Uniform Determination of Death Act (UDDA), approved in 1981 by the US and adopted by most states, the American Bar Association, and the American Medical Association, provides for a medically and legally sound basis for defining death that takes into consideration future technological advancements. It separates brain death from persistent vegetative state. In this regard, the UDDA approves of the irreversible function of the whole brain, which includes the higher brain (e.g., Madoff, 2011). Death of the whole brain also reflects the cessation of vital signs and functioning of the higher brain. However, the cessation of vital signs may not reflect death of the whole brain as exemplified from the scenarios reviewed earlier.

Variations to Defining Death

Belief systems and available medical technology are also influential in death definition across the world. In determining death, consideration should be given to personal beliefs and wishes. These are stated in an advance directive such as a living will or a do-not-resuscitate (DNR) order, which a doctor writes after talking with the patient (or the patient's surrogate) and does not include any plan for treatment or for palliative care (e.g., pain medication). For some individuals, a strong belief system is a more important factor in determining a death, even in the presence of good medical infrastructure. For others, however, available medical infrastructure is more important than a strong belief system in determining death.

In the cases reviewed earlier of people mistaken as dead, the issue did not appear to be a strong belief system nor unavailable medical infrastructure but of medical misjudgment, perhaps spurred by a quickness to decision. A mistaken death could be avoided if medical practitioners are slow to declare and certify a death. In some religions (e.g., Islam, Jewish) burials should occur within 24 hours. However, this should be after a death has been established. Former US president George Washington who died on December 14, 1799 allegedly made the following dying request: "Have me decently buried, but do not let my body be put into a vault in less than two days after I am dead" (Cavendish, 1999; https://www.historytoday.com/archive/death-george -washington).

George Washington's death was determined to be cardiopulmonary cessation or somatic observation and not cessation of brain functioning. Yet his timeframe of two days of wait time before burial is worthy of consideration in today's world. Some parts of the world still lack the facility for determining brain death using modern technology. To wait a while before declaring a person as dead, however, may impede organ donation, as time is of the essence. Yet, the action to retrieve an organ can only be taken after brain death has been established (Organdonor .gov, n.d.; https://www.organdonor.gov/about/process/deceased -donation .html).

CAUSES OF DEATH

Among nations of the world, there is a nexus between predominant causes of death and available resources. As highlighted in previous chapters, in resource-rich nations like the US, non-communicable diseases (e.g., heart disease and cancer) are the prevalent causes of death, whereas in resource-poor countries like Haiti, communicable diseases (e.g., diarrheal infection) are mostly responsible for death. However, with human movements infectious diseases can be transmitted across borders, allowing communicable diseases to have a global reach. As examples, the following are infectious diseases and their impacts in recent years:

- HIV/AIDS pandemic: By 2018 about 32 million (23.6-43.8 million) people have died from AIDS-related illnesses globally (https://www.unaids.org/en/resources/fact-sheet; 2019).

- SARS (Severe Acute Respiratory Syndrome) was first reported in Asia and subsequently spread to more than two dozen countries, including in North America, South America, and Europe, before it was contained in 2004 (https://www.cdc.gov/sars/index.html).
- COVD-19 (novel coronavirus): With origins in Asia in 2019, this disease has spread to every continent of the world and claimed over 750,000 lives by August 15, 2020 (Picheto, 2020; CNN: https://www.cnn.com/2020/05/14/world/coronavirus-global-death-toll-300000-intl/index.html).

According to the WHO (2004), infectious diseases are the second leading cause of death worldwide.

FUNERAL AND BURIAL PRACTICES

Around the world there are *conventional* and *unconventional* methods to funeral and burial practices. Unconventional methods are influenced by technology, sensitivity to the environment or declines in religiosity.

Conventional Methods

Conventional funeral practices include viewing of the dead body, visiting with the deceased's loved ones (at a funeral home or at the deceased's home) and including a eulogy for the deceased. Usually the deceased's body is embalmed in preparation for viewing. During funerals, rituals (religious rituals including prayers) highlight the afterlife journey of the deceased. Christians mention heaven (or hell), Muslims speak of paradise, and Hindus and Buddhists emphasize reincarnation. In the eulogy, the decedent's life provides a suggested location for the deceased in the afterlife and forms a basis for exhorting family and friends on how to live (or not to live) their own lives in preparation for the afterlife. Conventional burial practices include below or above ground burial (mausoleum), with the body placed in a casket or a container. A committal service is conducted at the graveside, usually with a religious flavor indicating the body's return to the dust from which it came. Christians are reminded of the wordings in the Bible in Genesis 2:7 that says: "And the LORD God formed man of the dust of the ground, and breathed into his nostrils the breath of life; and man became a living being" (New King James version).

Unconventional Methods

Unconventional funeral and burial practices are novel, being spurred by developments in technology, sensitivity to the environment, or declines in religiosity.

The use of technology that enables for webcasting or live streaming of funerals allows family and friends to participate remotely. Also, the move towards biodegradable caskets or coffins and cremation instead of earth burial allows for a cleaner environment. The "green" casket or coffin is made of plant-based materials such as bamboo, seagrass or banana leaves. Cremation does away with the need for a conventional burial casket/coffin or containment, as well. To reduce air pollution, there is a shift from combustible cremation to use of biochemicals that blends water with an alkaline solution of potassium hydroxide. This is added to the body in a pressurized stainless steel chamber, with the temperature raised to 350° F (e.g., Greencremation, n.d.; file:///Users/feyetsemitan/Downloads/understanding-green-cremation -brochure%20(2).pdf). In the US, cremation is relatively cheaper than burial. In 2020, the cost for a basic or direct cremation (excluding the cost of funeral) is between $800 and $3000, depending on the city you live in (Cremation Institute, n.d.; https://cremationinstitute .com/cremation-costs/). In contrast, in 2019 the median cost of a burial and viewing, including a vault required by a cemetery, is $9,135. And this excludes the cost of a cemetery lot and a monument or marker. Beginning in 2015, the National Funeral Directors Association (2019) illustrates a growing preference in the US for cremation over burial (see Figure 12.1). Cremation, however, is common among believers of Hinduism and Buddhism, who view it as expediting the release of the deceased's spirit after death (Hinduism Today, n.d.; https://www.hinduismtoday.com/modules/smartsection/item.php ?itemid=5676).

Generally, unconventionalists treat the decedent's body as separate from the decedent's life. Whereas the decedent's body is meant for burial, the decedent's life is to be celebrated or memorialized. In the burial of the decedent's body only a few people may participate (including close friends and family), but in the celebration or memo-

Figure 12.1
Percentage of Burial Use Versus Cremation Use, 2010- 2040

	2010 (final data)	2015 (final data)	2020 (projected data)	2025 (projected data)	2030 (projected data)	2035 (projected data)	2040 (projected data)
Burial (%)	53.3	45.2	37.5	30.6	24.6	19.6	15.7
Cremation (%)	40.4	47.9	56.4	63.5	69.7	74.8	78.7

Source: https://www.nfda.org/news/statistics

rialization of the decedent's life, more people are invited or expected to take part, including on media platforms. For example, former Los Angeles Lakers basketball great Kobe Bryant passed away on January 26, 2020 in an unfortunate helicopter crash. While the family had a private burial service for him (and his daughter Gianna who also was killed in the crash), a separate public memorial or funeral service was held at the Staples Center, where a celebration of his life/memory took place and beamed live on national television (e.g., Bengel, 2020; CBS Sports: https://www.cbssports.com/nba/news/kobe-bryant-gianna -bryant-buried-in-private-family-service-near-california-home/).

With declines in religiosity, especially in Europe and other parts of the world, funerals are now held in buildings outside of the church and officiated by persons other than the clergy. In Australia, a *funeral celebrant* who is a non-religious professional is used to officiate in funerals and is not obligated to prognosticate about the deceased's location in the afterlife. Unexpected deaths that overwhelm human resources can trigger unconventional means of funerals and burials, also. The COVID-19 is an example where, for many of its victims, no funeral was conducted because of the contagious nature of the disease. Usually funerals provide opportunities for friends and family to visit with the bereaved and show their support, but with COVID-19 this was made difficult due to social distancing and restrictions on the number of people who could congregate in order to reduce the spread of the disease. Prior to burial, traditional and religious rites could not take place, and loved ones were unable to touch, kiss or say their farewells, thus affecting the grieving process adversely (e.g., Amante, Hafezi & Choi, 2020; https://www.reuters.com/article/us-health

-coronavirus-rites-insight/there-are-no-funerals-death-in-quarantine
-leaves-nowhere-to-grieve-idUSKBN2161ZM).

EXPANDING ON GRIEF MODELS

Grief models serve as guideposts in helping with understanding, describing, predicting and intervening in behaviors of people who have lost loved ones or are going through the dying process. To have far-reaching global impacts, existing grief models may have to take into consideration the following:

Influences of Religion

In the teachings of the Islamic religion, occurrence of death is at the will of Allah (God), even if unexpected. Believers should accept Allah's will without questioning regarding death. Therefore, in the grief process believers of Islam begin with acceptance of a loss. Due to religious teachings, the *acceptance* of a loss is different than the *acknowledgement* of a loss. The acceptance of a loss is more cognitive and may not be followed with as much the pain that may accompany the acknowledgement of a loss which is more visual (e.g., from attending a funeral). Islam in 2015 has an estimated 1.8 billion followers around the world and about 24% of the world's population (Lipkar, 2017; Pew Research Center; https://www.pewresearch.org/fact-tank/2017/08/09/muslims-and-islam-key-findings-in-the-u-s-and-around-the-world/). In Kubler-Ross's (1969) stages of dying, the dying (or grieving) process ends with acceptance. However, with Muslims, if acceptance comes first, it would impact differently on Kubler-Ross's stages of denial, anger, bargaining and depression. After acceptance, would there be a subsequent denial, anger, bargaining or depression stage?

Conflicting Belief Systems

Conflicting belief systems arise from maintaining more than one belief system, e.g., Western and non-Western beliefs. Western medicine's autopsy report may help the survivor to accept the loss and adjust to the new environment created by the loss. William Worden's (2008) four tasks in mourning include accepting the loss, acknowledging the pain of the loss, adjusting to a new environment, and maintaining an enduring connection to the deceased while reinvesting in new relationships.

If Western medicine points to a scientific basis for the loss (e.g., cardiac arrest) but a non-Western belief system suggests to evil eye instead, it becomes a challenge in going through the grieving process. The conflicting beliefs as to the *cause* of death may have to be reconciled first (or the bereaved would have to hold on to both beliefs) in order to move on with the grieving process. If the beliefs are not reconciled (or both beliefs are held on to), the griever might *passively* cope with the new environment created by the loss rather than *actively* adjust to the new environment (based on a unidirectional firm understanding as to the cause of death). Although not a similar situation, reports that parents never get past the loss of a child, even almost 20 years after, holds a cognitive parallel. The bereaved parent could not make progress by *actively* adjusting to their new environment created by the loss of their child, perhaps due to conflicting beliefs. The child might have died of a medical illness such as cancer and acknowledged through an autopsy report; yet, the child's death is considered as "off-time" because of sociocultural/biological beliefs that parents should not outlive their children. Thus, a conflict in belief systems creates a stall in the grieving process. Researcher Catherine Rogers and colleagues (2008) reported on the long-term impact that the loss of a child could have on the lives of parents. In their study of 428 participants per group, when compared to parents of similar backgrounds, bereaved parents reported more depressive symptoms, poorer health, and poorer well-being over an average of 18.05 years after the loss of their child. In other words, bereaved parents are not adjusting well to the new environment created by their loss, perhaps due to conflicting belief systems.

Other-Centered

The focus of most grief models is on the bereaved person, including actions that the survivor needs to take to get back to normalcy after a loss. However, shifting attention to the deceased, instead, might help the bereaved with the grieving process. By doing things that the bereaved perceives would be pleasing to the deceased, the survivor might otherwise receive healing in the process. Lisa Farino (2010) notes that there is no shortage of research that points to the beneficial effects of focusing on others. In a study by researchers Carolyn Schwartz and Rabbi Meir Sendor (1999), lay people with a chronic disease were trained to provide compassionate, unconditional regard to others who had the same illness. The result showed that the providers of care and compassion reported better quality of life than the recipients of care and compassion, even though both givers and receivers had the same illness. The givers showed profound improvements in confidence, self-awareness, self-esteem, depression, and in role functioning. The researchers emphasized the beneficial importance of "response shift" (the shifting of internal standards, values, and concept definition of health and well-being) in dealing with one's own adverse situation. Farino (2010) notes that this research is profound because of the belief in Western culture that feeling happy tends to be getting something for yourself.

There may be biological origins to the notion that "it's better to give than to receive." Using the functional magnetic resonance imaging (fMRI), researchers were able to demonstrate a connection between brain activity and giving. People who gave voluntarily and also for a good cause experienced more activation of the part of brain that controls for pleasure and happiness (e.g., Harbaugh, Mayr, & Burghart, 2007). Researcher Stephen Post and colleague, Jill Neimark (2008), in their book, "Why Good Things Happen to Good People: How to Live a Longer, Healthier, Happier Life by the Simple Act of Giving," note that a way to alleviate stress is by doing good things for others, and for the deceased, as well, as suggested in the *deceased-focused approach* to bereavement.

Usually, survivors show concerns about how their deceased loved ones felt prior to death and whether they are happy or not in the after-life. In one study, respondents used emotion discrete terms such as sad, happy or angry to describe the faces of deceased persons, just like with living people. The researchers suggest that the perceived emotional state of the deceased, could affect the survivor's mourning trajectory (e.g., Eyetsemitan & Eggleston, 2002). However, the survivors' concerns could be alleviated knowing they are doing what would be pleasing to their deceased loved ones.

SUMMARY

1. How death is defined is worth understanding because of its finality. If death is poorly defined, this could lead to an error of "buried alive."
2. Over the years, the definition of death has changed with the discovery of new technology. Death's definition has been based on the following criteria:
   - *Somatic:* A visual inspection of the body without knowing details of the state of internal organs, e.g., decomposition of the body, decapitation or rigor mortis (stiffening of joints and muscles a few hours after death).
   - *Circulatory:* An irreversible cessation of circulatory and respiratory functions. A cardiopulmonary test on pulse or heartbeat and also of breath is the basis for making conclusions about death. This approach examines "vital signs."
   - *Neurological:* A brain test using an EEG, or electroencephalogram, to determine death.
3. The Uniform Determination of Death Act (UDDA), approved in 1981 by the US provides a medically and legally sound basis for defining death that takes into consideration technological advancements. It approves of the irreversible function of the whole brain, which includes the higher brain.
4. *Personal beliefs and wishes* could be used to determine death, e.g., advance directive such as a living will or a do-not-resuscitate (DNR) order.
5. Death determination differs from country to country based on available medical technology to determine brain death and belief systems.
6. At the individual level, for some people a strong belief system is more important even in the presence of good medical infrastructure, whereas for others a good medical infrastructure is more important than a strong belief system in determining death.
7. Among the nations of the world, the predominant causes of death vary according to resource availability. In rich nations like the US, non-communicable diseases (e.g., heart disease and cancer) are the more prevalent causes of death, whereas in resource-poor countries like Haiti communicable diseases

(e.g., diarrheal infection) make up the predominant cause of death.

8. With human movements, infectious diseases are transmissible across borders making communicable diseases such as COVID-19 to have a global reach.

9. Around the world there are *conventional* and *unconventional* methods to funeral and burial practices. Unconventional methods are being influenced by technology, sensitivity to the environment, or declines in religiosity.

10. Beginning in 2015 the National Funeral Directors Association (2019) illustrates a growing preference for cremation over burial in the US.

11. Grief models may take into consideration the following, in order to have far-reaching global effects:

    • Religion: in the teachings of the Islamic religion, believers should accept Allah's will without questioning regarding death. Therefore, for believers of Islam the grief process starts with acceptance of the loss. In Kubler-Ross's (1969) stages of dying the grieving/dying process ends with acceptance, instead.

    • Conflicting belief systems: Some people maintain more than one belief system, e.g., Western and non-Western beliefs, thereby affecting how would they proceed through the grief process.

    • Other-centered (as opposed to self-centered): Most grief models focus on the bereaved person, including actions the survivor needs to take to get back to normalcy. Shifting attention to the deceased instead might help the bereaved with the grieving process. Research points to the beneficial effects of focusing on others (rather than self) in producing happiness and getting through difficult times.

Key Terms

Burial
Buried alive
Conflicting belief systems
Conventional methods
Cremation

Infectious disease
Neurological
Organ donation
Other-centered
Personal beliefs and wishes
Religion
Response shift
Somatic
Unconventional methods
Vital signs

Review Questions

1. How would you define death?
2. Discuss your preference of burial and funeral methods
3. What factors should grief models consider to have a global reach?
4. Describe how the global impact of communicable diseases such as COVID-19 could be minimized
5. Why should grief models be "other-centered?"

Additional Readings

Stillion, J., & Attig, J. (Eds.). (2014). *Death, dying and bereavement: Contemporary perspectives, institutions and practices.* New York, NY: Springer.

GLOSSARY

Abiku: A person destined to die before reaching maturity among the Yoruba ethnic group of Nigeria.

Accommodation behavior: Maintaining both Western and non-Western value systems—a behavior found mostly among non-Western people.

Acquired self: A selfhood influenced by a foreign culture.

Alternative medicine: Treatment used as a replacement to Western medicine.

Ancestor worship: A religious practice based on the belief that deceased family members have a continued existence, that the spirits of deceased ancestors will look after the family, take an interest in the affairs of the world, and possess the ability to influence the fortune of the living.

Ancestor listening: Belief that ancestors could be listened to in spirit form.

Anticipatory grief: Grief that precedes an imminent loss.

Arranged marriage: A marriage in which spouses are chosen for each other by parents and relatives.

Bereavement: A state whereby someone has experienced a loss.

Collectivism versus Individualism: In collectivism, group values are more important, whereas in individualism personal values take precedent over group values.

Complicated grief: Grief that is persistent and does not go away.

Complementary medicine: Treatment used to augment Western medicine.

Candomble and Umbanda: Afro-Brazilian religions brought by black slaves from Africa.

Coping: Adjusting to changes brought about by a loss, including deploying both primary resources (e.g., explanatory styles) and secondary resources disposal (e.g., social support). Some manner of coping, however, can lead to maladjustment (e.g., use of drug or excessive use of alcohol).

Death culture: A society's common approach to death and dying.

Death doula: Someone who provides social, emotional, and practical support for dying persons (and their families). More importantly, the support is non-specific, but based on the dying person's needs.

Death tourism: To travel from a location with no assistance for the dying to a place where such is provided.

Deceased-focused approach to mourning: Placing emphasis on doing what is pleasing to the deceased, in helping with grief recovery.

Disenfranchised grief: Grief that is not recognized by others in a society.

"Duppies" or "jupies": Local names for spirits in Barbados.

Evil eye: A belief that certain people can put a spell on others that can cause them harm or lead to death.

Espiritismo: In Portuguese or Spanish, it is the belief that good and bad spirits are influencers in human life.

Funeral celebrant: In New Zealand, a paid professional with no religious affiliation, who conducts a funeral service in accordance with the values, beliefs and lifestyle of the deceased.

Grief: A normal reaction to a loss (e.g., physical, cognitive, emotional and spiritual).

Grief work: A bereaved person's efforts to break ties with the deceased and move on with life.

Group Self Esteem: A person's self-worth that is group based.

Libation: Drink poured to ancestors as offerings, usually on the floor or ground indicating earthly burial.

Marai: in New Zealand, a complex building that surrounds a courtyard for social events.

Mourning: The way a culture prescribes how to respond to a loss (e.g., funeral, burial rituals, normal length for grief).

Native Patient Navigator: An advocate for the health needs of ethnic minority people, based on cultural competence.

Native self: A selfhood influenced by an indigenous culture.

Ogbanje: A spirit that deliberately accurses a family with evil among the Ibo ethnic group of Nigeria.

Okwaabya olumbe: Among the Buganda of Uganda, the act of "destroying death" by engaging in post-bereavement celebrations

Proper burial: A burial that is done in accordance with the laid down tradition of indigenous people.

Santeria: The blending of Indigenous African religion with Roman Catholicism.

Sati: a practice in India whereby a widow chooses to die with her husband during cremation by jumping into the funeral pyre.

Spirit children: Children who came into this world to torment their parents because they die soon after birth.

Spiritual healing: Among Saudis, a form of healing based on recitation of verses of the Koran and the specific sayings of the Prophet Mohammed.

Stereotype threat: Occurs when a person's poor performance, behavior or thought patterns conform to negative societal expectations.

Traditional medical practice: A mixture of the cultural, social, psychological and spiritual elements of a people group, with healing as an outcome.

Triarchical environmental dimensions: A society's environmental dimension that comprises global, Western and non-Western aspects.

Velorios: In Hispanic, the wake that provides an occasion for friends and family members to gather and reflect on their relationships with the deceased and pay their condolences.

Verbal autopsy: An autopsy report on death causation not based on science but on how the deceased behaved prior to death.

Vodou (or Voodoo): An Afro-Haitian religion that has a spiritual explanation for everything including death, illness or justice.

REFERENCES

Adeyemo, T. (1979). *Salvation in African traditional religion.* Nairobi: Evangel Publishing House.

Al-Shahri, M. Z. (2002). Culturally sensitive caring for Saudi patients. *Journal of Transcultural Nursing, 13*(2), 133–138.

Amante, A., Hafezi, P., & Choi, H. (2020): *'There are no funerals:' Death in quarantine leaves nowhere to grieve.* https://www.reuters.com/article/us-health-coronavirus-rites -insight/there-are-no-funerals-death-in-quarantine-leaves-nowhere-to-grieve -idUSKBN2161ZM

American Medical Association. (n.d.). *Physician-assisted suicide.* https://www.ama-assn .org/delivering-care/ethics/physician-assisted-suicide/

American Psychological Association. (n.d.). *Personality.* https://www.apa.org/topics /personality/

Annadurai, K., Danasekaran, R., & Mani, G. (2014). Euthanasia: right to die with dignity. *Journal of Family Medicine and Primary Care, 3*(4), 477–478.

Anderson, J. E. (2015). *The voodoo encyclopedia: Magic, ritual, and religion: Magic, ritual, and religion.* ABC-CLIO.

Antoni, M. H., Lutgendorf, S. K., Cole, S. W., Dhabhar, F. S., Sephton, S. E., McDonald, P. G., Stefanek, M., & Sood, A. K. (2006). The influence of biobehavioural factors on tumour biology: Pathways and mechanisms. *Nature Reviews Cancer, 6*(3), 240–248.

Atkins, J. (2012). Class acts and daredevils: Black masculinity in jazz funeral dancing. *The Journal of American Culture, 35*(2), 166.

Australian Bureau of Statistics. (2020). *Population Clock.* https://www.abs.gov.au /ausstats/abs%40.nsf/94713ad445ff1425ca25682000192af2/1647509ef7e25faaca 2568a900154b63?OpenDocument/

Australian Bureau of Statistics. (2010). *Causes of Death, Australia.* https://www.abs.gov .au/ausstats/abs@.nsf/Products/6BAD463E482C6970CA2579C6000F6AF7 ?opendocument/

Baetz, M., & Bowen, R. (2008). Chronic pain and fatigue: Associations with religion and spirituality. *Pain Research and Management, 13*(5), 383–388.

Baider, L., & Goldzweig, G. (2016). A brief encounter with the middle east: A narrative of one muslim woman diagnosed with breast cancer. *Asia-Pacific Journal of Oncology Nursing, 3*(2), 205.

Baloyi, L. (2009). *Psychology and psychotherapy redefined from the viewpoint of the African experience.* http://uir.unisa.ac.za/handle/10500/1346/

Bandura, A., & Walters, R. H. (1977). *Social learning theory*. Englewood Cliffs, NJ: Prentice-Hall.

Baptist, K. W. (2010). Diaspora: Death without a landscape. *Mortality, 15*(4), 294–307.

Barlow, C., & Wineti, E. (1991). *Tikanga whakaaro: Key concepts in maori culture*. Auckland, New Zealand: Oxford University Press.

Bauer-Wu, S., Barrett, R., & Yeager, K. (2007). Spiritual perspectives and practices at the end-of-life: A review of the major world religions and application to palliative care. *Indian Journal of Palliative Care, 13*(2), 53.

Baumgartner, H., & Gerstenbrand, F. (2002). Diagnosing Brain Death without a Neurologist: Simple Criteria and Training are Needed for the Non-Neurologist in Many Countries. *BMJ, 324*(7352), 1471–1472.

BBC. (2017). *Nigeria's President Buhari travels to London for treatment*. https://www.bbc.com/news/world-africa-39842686/

BBC. (2013). *How many Roman Catholics are there in the world?* https://www.bbc.com/news/world-21443313/

BBC. (2009). *Christian funerals*. https://www.bbc.co.uk/religion/religions/christianity/ritesrituals/funerals.shtml

Beasley, N. M. (2009). *Christian ritual and the creation of British slave societies, 1650–1780*. University of Georgia Press.

Bengel, C. (2020). *Cbssports; Kobe Bryant, Gianna Bryant buried in private family service near California home*. https://www.cbssports.com/nba/news/kobe-bryant-gianna-bryant-buried-in-private-family-service-near-california-home/

Berry, J. W. (1997). Immigration, acculturation, and adaptation. *Applied Psychology, 46*(1), 5–34.

Berry, J. W. (2006). Contexts of acculturation. In D. L. Sam & J. W. Berry (Eds.), *The Cambridge handbook of acculturation psychology* (pp. 27–42). Cambridge University Press.

Bilikiewicz, A., Puzynski, S., Rybakowski, J., & Wiórka, J. (2002). *Clinical Psychiatry*. Vol. 1. Wroclaw: Medical Publisher Urban & Partner.

Billing, T. K., Bhagat, R., Babakus, E., Srivastava, B. N., Shin, M., & Brew, F. (2014). Work–family conflict in four national contexts: A closer look at the role of individualism–collectivism. *International Journal of Cross Cultural Management, 14*(2), 139–159.

Black, M. J., & Yacoob, Y. (1995). Tracking and recognizing rigid and non-rigid facial motions using local parametric models of image motion. Paper presented at the *Proceedings of IEEE International Conference on Computer Vision*, 374–381.

Black, M. J., & Yacoob, Y. (1997). Recognizing facial expressions in image sequences using local parameterized models of image motion. *International Journal of Computer Vision, 25*(1), 23–48.

Black, R. E., Morris, S. S., & Bryce, J. (2003). Where and why are 10 million children dying every year? *The Lancet, 361*(9376), 2226–2234.

Bonanno, G. A., Wortman, C. B., Lehman, D. R., Tweed, R. G., Haring, M., Sonnega, J., Carr, D., & Nesse, R. M. (2002). Resilience to loss and chronic grief: A prospective study from preloss to 18-months postloss. *Journal of Personality and Social Psychology, 83*(5), 1150.

Bostwick, H. (n.d.). *10 famous people who died without a will.* https://www.legal zoom.com/articles/10-famous-people-who-died-without-a-will/

Bousso, R. S., Poles, K., Serafim, T. d. S., & Miranda, M. G. (2011). Religious beliefs, illness and death: Family's perspectives in illness experience. *Rev Esc Enferm USP, 45*(2), 397–403.

Boustan, R. S. (2004). Angels in the architecture: Temple art and the poetics of praise in the "songs of the sabbath sacrifice." *Heavenly Realms and Earthly Realities in Late Antique Religions,* 195–212.

Braun, K. L., & Nichols, R. (1997). Death and dying in four Asian American cultures: A descriptive study. *Death Studies, 21*(4), 327.

Braun, K. L., Pietsch, J. H., & Blanchette, P. L. (1999). (Eds.). *Cultural issues in end-of-life decision making.* Sage Publications.

Britannica.com. (n.d.). *Four noble truths.* https://www.britannica.com/topic/Four -Noble-Truths/

Brittanica.com. (n.d.). *Latin America.* https://www.britannica.com/topic/race -human/Latin-America/

Britannica.com. (n.d.). *Islam.* https://www.britannica.com/topic/Islam/

Brittanica.com. (n.d). *Pacific islands/early period.* https://www.britannica.com /place/Pacific-Islands/Early-period

Britannica.com. (n.d.). *Suriname.* https://www.britannica.com/place/Suriname /People/

Brooks, L. J., Haskins, D. G., & Kehe, J. V. (2004). Counseling and psychotherapy with African American clients. *Practicing Multiculturalism: Affirming Diversity in Counseling and Psychology,* 145–166.

Bureau of Statistics, Guyana. (2016). *Guyana 2012 census compendium 2.* https://www .google.com/search?q=Guyana+2012+census+compendium+2.&oq=Guyana +2012+census+compendium+2.&aqs=chrome..69i57j33l4.1413j0j7&sourceid =chrome&ie=UTF-8/

Burhansstipanov, L., Krebs, L. U., Dignan, M. B., Jones, K., Harjo, L. D., Watanabe-Galloway, D. G., Petereit, N. L., & Pingatore, D. I. (2014). Findings from the native navigators and the cancer continuum (NNACC) study. *Journal of Cancer Education, 29*(3), 420–427.

Caffaro, F., Ferraris, F., & Schmidt, S. (2014). Gender differences in the perception of honour killing in individualist versus collectivistic cultures: Comparison between Italy and Turkey. *Sex Roles, 71*(9-10), 296–318.

Cavendish, R. (1999). History Today. *The death of George Washington.* https://www .historytoday.com/archive/death-george-washington).

Center for Disease Control and Prevention. (2016). *Changes in Life Expectancy by Race and Hispanic Origin in the United States, 2013–2014.* https://www.cdc.gov/nchs /products/databriefs/db244.htm/

Center for Disease Control and Prevention. (n.d.). *Severe acute respiratory syndrome (SARS).* https://www.cdc.gov/sars/index.html/

Center for Disease Control and Prevention. (n.d.). *Coping with stress.* https://www.cdc .gov/violenceprevention/suicide/copingwith-stresstips.html/

Chabad.org. (n.d.). *Why does Judaism forbid cremation?* https://www.chabad.org /library/article_cdo/aid/510874/jewish/Why-Does-Judaism-Forbid-Cremation .htm/

Chachkes, E., & Jennings, R. (1994). Latino communities: Coping with death. In B. Dane & C. Levine (Eds.), *AIDS and the new orphans: Coping with death* (pp. 77–99). Westport, CT: Auburn House/Greenwood Publishing Group.

Chan, C. L. W., & Chow, A. Y. M. (2006). *Death, dying and bereavement: A Hong Kong Chinese experience.* Hong Kong University Press.

Chan, C. L., Chow, A. Y., Ho, S. M., Tsui, Y. K., Tin, A. F., Koo, B. W., & Koo, E. W. (2005). The experience of Chinese bereaved persons: A preliminary study of meaning making and continuing bonds. *Death Studies, 29*(10), 923–947.

Chestnut, R. A. (2003). Pragmatic consumers and practical products: The success of pneumacentric religion among women in Latin America's new religious economy. *Review of Religious Research,* 20–31.

Christensen, K., Doblhammer, G., Rau, R., & Vaupel, J. W. (2009). Ageing populations: The challenges ahead. *The Lancet, 374*(9696), 1196–1208.

CIA. (n.d.). *The World Factbook. Library.* https://www.cia.gov/library/publications /the-world-factbook/geos/ha.html)

CIA. (n.d.). *The World Factbook. South America-Colombia.* https://www.cia.gov/library /publications/the-worldfactbook/geos/co.html: South America-Colombia/ (updated June 16, 2020).

Clements, P. T., Vigil, G. J., Manno, M. S., Henry, G. C., Wilks, J., Das, S., Kellywood, R., & Foster, W. (2003). Cultural perspectives of death, grief, and bereavement. *Journal of Psychosocial Nursing and Mental Health Services, 41*(7), 18–26.

Colclough, Y. Y. (2016). Native American death taboo: Implications for health care providers. *American Journal of Hospice and Palliative Medicine;* 1–8.

Conserve Africa. (2002). Pambazuka News. *Africa: Overview on Medicinal Plants and Traditional Medicine.* https://www.pambazuka.org/food-health/africa-overview -medicinal-plants-and-traditional-medicine

Counts, D. A., & Counts, D. R. (1985). I'm not dead yet! Aging and death: Process and experience in Kaliai. In *Aging and its Transformations: Moving Toward Death in Pacific Societies* (pp. 131–156). Pittsburgh: University of Pittsburgh Press.

Cremation Institute. (n.d.). *Cremation cost guide.* https://cremationinstitute.com /cremation-costs/https://www.nfda.org/news/statistics/

Cross-roads Hospice & Palliative Care. (2017). *All you need to know about pain management in hospice.* https://www.crossroadshospice.com/hospice-palliative-care -blog/2017/september/07/all-you-need-to-know-about-pain-management-in -hospice/;

Culling, V., & Mitchell, P. (2015). Ahakoa he iti, he pounamu: Although small, it is precious: Death and grief after perinatal death in Aotearoa/New Zealand. In J. Cacciatore & J. DeFrain (Eds.), *The world of bereavement* (pp. 265–286). New York: Springer.

Cusick, J. (2003). Spirituality and voluntary pain. *APS Bulletin, 13*(5), 3–5.

Dallman, M. F., Pecoraro, N., Akana, S. F., La Fleur, S. E., Gomez, F., Houshyar, H., Bell, M.E., Bhatnagar, S., Laugero, K.D., & Manalo, S. (2003). Chronic stress and obesity: A new view of "comfort food." *Proceedings of the National Academy of Sciences, 100*(20), 11696–11701.

Daly, N. (2005). *Sasha's legacy: A guide to funerals for babies.* Wellington, NZ: Steele Roberts Limited.

Dantzer, R., O'Connor, J. C., Freund, G. G., Johnson, R. W., & Kelley, K. W. (2008). From inflammation to sickness and depression: When the immune system subjugates the brain. *Nature Reviews Neuroscience, 9*(1), 46–56.

Davis, N. (2019). *Euthanasia and assisted dying rates are soaring. But where are they legal?* https://www.theguardian.com/news/2019/jul/15/euthanasia-and-assisted-dying-rates-are-soaring-but-where-are-they-legal;

Davies, R. (2004). New understandings of parental grief: Literature review. *Journal of Advanced Nursing, 46,* 506–512.

Dearden, L. (2014). *'Dead' three-year-old girl wakes up in coffin at her own funeral in Philippines.* Independent. https://www.independent.co.uk/news/world/asia/dead-three-year-old-girl-wakes-up-in-coffin-at-her-own-funeral-in-philippines-9604875.html/

de Greef, K. (2018). New York Times. *She Was Declared Dead and Moved to the Morgue. Then She Was Heard Breathing.* https://www.nytimes.com/2018/07/02/world/africa/south-africa-wrongly-declared-dead.html/

De La Torre, M. (2004). *Santería.* Grand Rapids, MI: Wm. B. Eerdmans Publishing Co.

Dedeli, O., & Kaptan, G. (2013). Spirituality and religion in pain and pain management. *Health Psychology Research, 1*(3).

Del Sarto, R. A. (2014). Israel and the European union: Between rhetoric and reality.

Diaz-Cabello, N. (2004). The Hispanic way of dying: Three families, three perspectives, three cultures. *Illness, Crisis & Loss, 12*(3), 239–255.

Doka, K. J. (1987). Silent sorrow: Grief and the loss of significant others. *Death Studies, 11*(6), 455–469.

Doka, K. J. (2002). *Disenfranchised grief: New directions, challenges, and strategies for practice.* Research Press Publication.

Doka, K. J., & Martin, T. L. (2011). *Grieving beyond gender: Understanding the ways men and women mourn.* Routledge.

Dong, H., & Zhang, X. (2001). An overview of traditional Chinese Medicine. In R. R. Chaudhury, & U. M. Rafel (Eds.), *Traditional Medicine in Asia* (pp. 17–30). New Delhi: World Health Organization (WHO).

Du Toit, B. M. (2001). Ethnomedical (folk) healing in the Caribbean. In M. F. Olmos, & L. Paravisini-Gebert (Eds.), *Healing cultures* (pp. 19–28). New York: Palgrave Macmillan.

Dwarakanath, C. (1970). Some significant aspects of the origin and development of medicine in ancient India. *Indian Journal of History of Science, 30*(5):1–12.

Eforms. (n.d). *Living Will Forms (Advance Directive).* https://eforms.com/living-will/

Ekman, P., & Friesen, W. V. (1986). A new pan-cultural facial expression of emotion. *Motivation and Emotion, 10*(2), 159–168.

El-Hazmi, M., & Warsy, A. S. (1997). Prevalence of obesity in the Saudi population. *Annals of Saudi Medicine, 17*(3), 302–306.

El-Kurd, M. (2012). *Cultural Diversity and Caring for Patients from the Middle East.* https://www.pcqn.org/wp-content/uploads/2012/11/Sept-Call_Cultural -Diversity-and-Caring-For-Patients-From-Middle-East.pdf/

Elliott, H. (2011). Moving beyond the medical model. *Journal of Holistic Healthcare, 8*(1).

Emanuel, E. J., Onwuteaka-Philipsen, B. D., Urwin, J. W., & Cohen, J. (2016). Attitudes and practices of euthanasia and physician-assisted suicide in the united states, Canada, and Europe. *JAMA, 316*(1), 79–90.

Erickson, E. H. (1958). *Young man Luther: A study in psychoanalysis and history.* New York: Norton.

Erikson, E. H. (1963). *Youth: Change and challenge.* New York: Basic books.

Essien, E. D. (2013). Notions of healing and transcendence in the trajectory of African traditional religion: Paradigm and strategies. *International Review of Mission, 102*(2), 236–248.

Estonica.org. (n.d.). *Death.* http://www.estonica.org/en/Culture/Traditional_folk _culture/Death/

Euthanasia.procon.org. (2019). *State-by-state physician-assisted suicide statistics.* https: //euthanasia.procon.org/state-by-state-physician-assisted-suicide-statistics/

Euthanasia.procon.org. (2016). *Euthanasia & Physician-Assisted Suicide around the world.* https://euthanasia.procon.org/euthanasia-physician-assisted-suicide -around-the-world

Eyetsemitan, F. (1998). Stifled grief in the workplace. *Death Studies, 22*(5), 469–479.

Eyetsemitan, F. E., & Gire, J. T. (2003). *Aging and adult development in the developing world: Applying Western theories and concepts.* Westport, CT: Greenwood Publishing Group.

Eyetsemitan, F., & Eggleston, T. (2002). The faces of deceased persons as emotion-expressive behaviors: Implications for mourning trajectories. *OMEGA-Journal of Death and Dying, 44*(2), 151–167.

Farino, L. (2010). Do good, feel good: New research shows that helping others may be the key to happiness. *MSN Healthy Living, March,* 7.

Festinger, L. (1957). *A theory of cognitive dissonance.* Stanford, CA: Stanford University Press.

Field, N. P. (2008). Whether to relinquish or maintain a bond with the deceased. In M. S. Stroebe, R. O. Hansson, H. Schut, & W. Stroebe (Eds.), *Handbook of bereavement research and practice: Advances in theory and intervention* (pp. 113–132). Washington, D.C.: American Psychological Association. https://doi.org/10 .1037/14498-006

Finkelstein, M. A. (2012). Individualism/collectivism and organizational citizenship behavior: An integrative framework. *Social Behavior and Personality: An International Journal, 40*(10), 1633–1643.

Firth, S. (2005). End-of-life: A Hindu view. *The Lancet, 366*(9486), 682–686.

Fischer, S., Min, S., Kline, D., & Fink, R. (2017). Apoyo con cariño: Patient navigation to improve palliative care outcomes for Latinos with advanced cancer (SA508B). *Journal of Pain and Symptom Management, 53*(2), 396–397.

Foster, T. L., Roth, M., Contreras, R., Gilmer, M. J., & Gordon, J. E. (2012). Continuing bonds reported by bereaved individuals in Ecuador. *Bereavement Care, 31*(3), 120–128.

Fottrell, E., Tollman, S., Byass, P., Golooba-Mutebi, F., & Kahn, K. (2012). The epidemiology of 'bewitchment' as a lay-reported cause of death in rural south Africa. *J Epidemiol Community Health, 66*(8), 704–709.

Frass, M., Strassl, R. P., Friehs, H., Müllner, M., Kundi, M., & Kaye, A. D. (2012). Use and acceptance of complementary and alternative medicine among the general population and medical personnel: A systematic review. *Ochsner Journal, 12*(1), 45–56.

Frazier, C., Mintz, L. B., & Mobley, M. (2005). A multidimensional look at religious involvement and psychological well-being among urban elderly African Americans. *Journal of Counseling Psychology, 52*(4), 583.

Freud, S. (1952). Thoughts for the times on war and death (E. C. Mayne, trans.). *The Major Works of Sigmund Freud, 54*, 755–766.

Gander, K. (2014). *Walter Williams dead: US man who woke up in a body bag dies two weeks later.* https://www.independent.co.uk/news/world/americas/walter-williams-dead-us-man-who-woke-up-in-a-body-bag-dies-two-weeks-later-9191156.html/

Garrett, M. T., Torres-Rivera, E., Brubaker, M., Portman, T. A. A., Brotherton, D., West-Olatunji, C., Conwill, W., & Grayshield, L. (2011). Crying for a vision: The Native American sweat lodge ceremony as therapeutic intervention. *Journal of Counseling & Development, 89*(3), 318–325.

Gervais, K. G. (1989). Advancing the definition of death: A philosophical essay. *Medical Humanities Review, 3*(2), 7.

Gillies, J., & Neimeyer, R. A. (2006). Loss, grief, and the search for significance: Toward a model of meaning reconstruction in bereavement. *Journal of Constructivist Psychology, 19*(1), 31–65.

Goldin, P. R., McRae, K., Ramel, W., & Gross, J. J. (2008). The neural bases of emotion regulation: Reappraisal and suppression of negative emotion. *Biological Psychiatry, 63*(6), 577–586.

Goldsmith, B., Morrison, R. S., Vanderwerker, L. C., & Prigerson, H. G. (2008). Elevated rates of prolonged grief disorder in African Americans. *Death Studies, 32*(4), 352–365.

Gottlieb, E. (2006). Development of religious thinking. *Religious Education, 101*(2), 242–260.

Government of New Zealand. (n.d.). *Maori values.* https://www.newzealandnow.govt.nz/living-in-nz/settling-in/maori-culture

Government of New Zealand. (n.d.). *Population.* https://www.stats.govt.nz/topics/population;

Graham, N., Gwyther, L., Tiso, T., & Harding, R. (2013). Traditional healers' views of the required processes for a "good death" among Xhosa patients pre-and post-death. *Journal of Pain and Symptom Management, 46*(3), 386–394.

GreenCremation.Com. (n.d.). *Understanding green cremation.* file:///Users/feyetsemitan/Downloads/understanding-green-cremation-brochure%20(2).pdf/

Hall, C. (2011). Beyond Kubler-Ross: Recent developments in our understanding of grief and bereavement. *InPsych: The Bulletin of the Australian Psychological Society Ltd, 33*(6), 8.

Hamilton, J. L., Potter, C. M., Olino, T. M., Abramson, L. Y., Heimberg, R. G., & Alloy, L. B. (2016). The temporal sequence of social anxiety and depressive symptoms following interpersonal stressors during adolescence. *Journal of Abnormal Child Psychology, 44*(3), 495–509.

Hampton, M., Baydala, A., Bourassa, C., McKay-McNabb, K., Placsko, C., Goodwill, K., McKenna, B., McNabb, P., & Boekelder, R. (2010). Completing the circle: Elders speak about end-of-life care with aboriginal families in Canada. *Journal of Palliative Care, 26*(1), 6–14.

Harbaugh, W. T., Mayr, U., & Burghart, D. R. (2007). Neural responses to taxation and voluntary giving reveal motives for charitable donations. *Science, 316*(5831), 1622–1625.

Harvard Health Publishing. (2018, May 1). *Understanding the stress response.* https://www.health.harvard.edu/staying-healthy/understanding-the-stress-response/

Heapost, L. (2007). The cemetery of Siksälä: Osteological and paleodemographical analysis. In S. Laul and H. Valk (Eds.), Siksälä: *A Community at the Frontiers. Iron Age and Medieval.* (CCC Papers, 10.) University of Tartu, Institute of History and Archaeology, Gotland University College, Centre for Baltic Studies, Tallinn, p. 213.

Heckhausen, J., & Schulz, R. (1995). A life-span theory of control. *Psychological Review, 102*(2), 284–304. https://doi.org/10.1037/0033-295X.102.2.284

Hedayat, K. (2006). When the spirit leaves: Childhood death, grieving, and bereavement in Islam. *Journal of Palliative Medicine, 9*(6), 1282–1291.

Heider, F. (1958). *The psychology of interpersonal relations.* New York: John Wiley.

Hilbrecht, M., Lero, D. S., Schryer, E., Mock, S. E., & Smale, B. (2017). Understanding the association between time spent caregiving and well-being among employed adults: Testing a model of work-life fit and sense of community. *Community, Work & Family, 20*(2), 162–180.

Hinduism Today. (n.d.). *Death and dying.* https://www.hinduismtoday.com/modules/smartsection/item.php?itemid=1667

Hinduism Today. (n.d.). *Why do Hindus cremate the dead?* https://www.hinduismtoday.com/modules/smartsection/item.php?itemid=5676/

Hines, P. M. (1991). Death and African-American culture. *Living Beyond Loss: Death in the Family,* 186–191.

History.co.uk. *Death rituals and superstitions.* https://www.history.co.uk/history-of-death/death-rituals-and-superstitions/

Hobfoll, S. E., Dunahoo, C. L., Ben-Porath, Y., & Monnier, J. (1994). Gender and coping: The dual-axis model of coping. *American Journal of Community Psychology, 22*(1), 49–82.

Hofmann, S. G., & Hay, A. C. (2018). Rethinking avoidance: Toward a balanced approach to avoidance in treating anxiety disorders. *Journal of Anxiety Disorders, 55,* 14–21.

Hofstede, G. (1980). *Culture's consequences: National differences in thinking and organizing.* Beverly Hills, CA: Sage.

Horowitz, J. (2016). New York Times. *For Donald Trump, Lessons from a Brother's Suffering.* https://www.nytimes.com/2016/01/03/us/politics/for-donald-trump-lessons -from-a-brothers-suffering.html/

Hsieh, D. H. (2002). Buddhism: China. *Encyclopedia of Modern Asia, 1,* 337–341.

Hsu, C., O'Connor, M., & Lee, S. (2009). Understandings of death and dying for people of Chinese origin. *Death Studies, 33*(2), 153–174.

Huggins, C. L., & Hinkson, G. M. (2019). Contemporary burial practices in three Caribbean islands among Christians of African descent. *OMEGA-Journal of Death and Dying, 80*(2), 266–279.

Hui, V. K., & Coleman, P. G. (2012). Do reincarnation beliefs protect older adult Chinese Buddhists against personal death anxiety? *Death Studies, 36*(10), 949–958.

Independent. (2012). *Man declared dead wakes up at his funeral in Egypt.* https://www .independent.co.uk/news/world/africa/man-declared-dead-wakes-up-at-his -funeral-in-egypt-7742041.html

International End of Life Doula Association (INELDA). (n.d.). *Professional Training & Coaching.* https://www.linkedin.com/company/international-end-of-life-doula -association-inedla-

Ireson, R., Sethi, B., & Williams, A. (2018). Availability of caregiver-friendly workplace policies (CFWP s): An international scoping review. *Health & Social Care in the Community, 26*(1), e1–e14.

Iso, H., Date, C., Yamamoto, A., Toyoshima, H., Tanabe, N., Kikuchi, S., Kondo, T., Wtanabe, Y., Wada, Y., Ishibashi, T., Suzuki, H., Koizumi, A., Inaba, Y., Tamakoshi, A., Ohno, Y., & JACC Study Group. (2002). Perceived mental stress and mortality from cardiovascular disease among Japanese men and women: The Japan collaborative cohort study for evaluation of cancer risk sponsored by monbusho (JACC study). *Circulation, 106*(10), 1229–1236.

Israel Central Bureau of Statistics. (2019). *Israel's Independence Day 2019.* Israel Central Bureau of Statistics. 6 May 2019.

Jewishfuneralguide.com. (n.d.). *Jewish burial society.* http://www.jewish-funeral-guide .com/tradition/chevra-kadisha.htm;

Jing Yin. (2006). Death from the Buddhist view: Knowing the unknown. In Chan, Cecilia Lai Wan, & Chow, Amy Yin Man (Eds.), *Death, dying and bereavement, A Hong Kong Chinese experience* (Vol. I). Hong Kong: Hong Kong University Press. pp. 93–104.

Jones, D. G. (1998). The problematic symmetry between brain birth and brain death. *Journal of Medical Ethics, 24*(4), 237–242.

Jones, K. (2015). It is normal to remember: Death and grief in Australia. In J. Cacciatore & J. DeFrain (Eds.) *The world of bereavement: cultural perspectives on death in families* (pp. 243–263). New York: Springer.

Joseph, S. E. (1995). *Coast Salish perceptions of death and dying: An ethnographic study* (Unpublished Master's thesis). University of Victoria, British Columbia.

Ka'ai, T. M., & R. Higgins. (2004). Te ao Maori: Maori world-view. In T. M. Ka'ai, J. C. Moorfield, M. P. Reilly, & S. Mosley (Eds.), *Ki Te Whaiao: An introduction to Maori culture and society* (pp. 13–25). Auckland: Pearson-Longman.

Ka'Ai, T. (2004). *Introduction to Maori culture and society*. Longman.

Kassin, S., Fein, S., & Markus, H. R. (2013). *Social psychology*. Nelson Education.

Kay, J., & Tasman, A. (2006). *Essentials of psychiatry*. John Wiley & Sons, Ltd.

Kemp, C., & Chang, B. (2002). Culture and the end of life: Chinese. *Journal of Hospice & Palliative Nursing, 4*(3), 173–178.

Kersting, A., Brähler, E., Glaesmer, H., & Wagner, B. (2011). Prevalence of complicated grief in a representative population-based sample. *Journal of Affective Disorders, 131*(1-3), 339–343.

King, M. (2003). *The penguin history of New Zealand*. Penguin Random House New Zealand Limited.

King, R. (2013). *Orientalism and religion: Post-colonial theory, India and "the mystic east."* Routledge.

Kitayama, S., Mesquita, B., & Karasawa, M. (2006). Cultural affordances and emotional experience: Socially engaging and disengaging emotions in Japan and the United States. *Journal of Personality and Social Psychology, 91*(5), 890.

Klass, D., Silverman, P. R., & Nickman, S. L. (1996). *Continuing bonds: New understandings of grief*. Abingdon, Oxford, England: Taylor & Francis.

Kleeman, T. F. (2003). Taoism. *Macmillan Encyclopedia of Death and Dying, 2*, 873–875.

Kochanek, K. D., Murphy, S. L., Anderson, R. N., & Scott, C. (2004). Deaths: Final data for 2002. *National Vital Statistics Report, 53*(5); 1–115.

Kristiansen, M., & Sheikh, A. (2012). Understanding faith considerations when caring for bereaved Muslims. *Journal of the Royal Society of Medicine, 105*(12), 513–517.

Kubler-Ross, E. (1969). *On death and dying*. New York: Macmillan.

Lanre-Abass, B. A. (2008). Cultural issues in advance directives relating to end of life decision making. *Prajna Vihara J Philos, 9:*23–49.

Laurie, A., & Neimeyer, R. A. (2008). African Americans in bereavement: Grief as a function of ethnicity. *Omega-Journal of Death and Dying, 57*(2), 173–193.

Lazar, N. M., Shemie, S., Webster, G. C., & Dickens, B. M. (2001). Bioethics for clinicians: 24. brain death. *CMAJ, 164*(6), 833–836.

Lehrer, J. A., Shrier, L. A., Gortmaker, S., & Buka, S. (2006). Depressive symptoms as a longitudinal predictor of sexual risk behaviors among US middle and high school students. *Pediatrics, 118*(1), 189–200.

Lichtenstein, A. H., Berger, A., & Cheng, M. J. (2017). Definitions of healing and healing interventions across different cultures. *Annals of Palliative Medicine, 6*(3), 248–252.

Lipkar, M. (2017). *Muslim and Islam: key findings in the U.S. and around the world*. Pew Research Center. https://www.pewresearch.org/fact-tank/2017/08/09/muslims-and-islam-key-findings-in-the-u-s-and-around-the-world/

Lipner, J. (2012). *Hindus: Their religious beliefs and practices*. Routledge.

Lo, Y. C. (1999). The relationship between the Taoist school and Taoism. *Journal of Chang Gung Institute of Nursing, 1*, 145–154.

Lobar, S. L., Youngblut, J. M., & Brooten, D. (2006). Cross-cultural beliefs, ceremonies, and rituals surrounding death of a loved one. *Pediatric Nursing, 32*(1), 44–50.

Loorits, O. (1949). Writings published by the Royal. Gustav Adolfs Academy of Public Life Research. *Grundzüge Des Estnischen Volksglaubens, 1,* 326.

Los Andes. (2017). *They were watching him, they realized he was breathing and they took him to the hospital.* https://www.losandes.com.ar/article/view?slug=lo-estaban -velando-se-dieron-cuenta-de-que-respiraba-y-lo-llevaron-al-hospital/

Lugira, A. M. (2009). *African traditional religion.* New York, NY: Chelsea House Publishing.

Maboea, S. I. (2002). *The influence of life-giving power in the African traditional religion and the Zionist churches in Soweto: A comparative study.* CB Powell Bible Centre, UNISA.

Madoff, R. (2011). How the law constructs its understanding of death. In V. Talwar, P. L. Harris, & M. Schleifer (Eds.), *Children's understanding of death: From biological to religious conceptions* (p. 156). Cambridge, UK: Cambridge University Press.

Manning, S. (2012). *Eco Burials Wellington. Funeralcare, Issue 35.* Wellington: Funeral Directors Association of New Zealand.

Marshall, R., & Sutherland, P. (2008). The social relations of bereavement in the Caribbean. *OMEGA-Journal of Death and Dying, 57*(1), 21–34.

Masel, E. K., Schur, S., & Watzke, H. H. (2012). Life is uncertain. Death is certain. Buddhism and palliative care. *Journal of Pain and Symptom Management, 44*(2), 307–312.

Mathur, M. B., Epel, E., Kind, S., Desai, M., Parks, C. G., Sandler, D. P., & Khazeni, N. (2016). Perceived stress and telomere length: A systematic review, meta-analysis, and methodologic considerations for advancing the field. *Brain, Behavior, and Immunity, 54,* 158–169.

Maynard, B. (2014). *My right to death with dignity at 29.* https://www.cnn.com/2014 /10/07/opinion/maynard-assisted-suicide-cancer-dignity)

McRae, K., Hughes, B., Chopra, S., Gabrieli, J. D., Gross, J. J., & Ochsner, K. N. (2010). The neural bases of distraction and reappraisal. *Journal of Cognitive Neuroscience, 22*(2), 248–262.

Mead, H. M. (2016). *Tikanga Maori: Living by Maori values* (Rev. ed.). Thorndon, Wellington, New Zealand: HUIA publishers.

Mehraby, N. (2003). Psychotherapy with Islamic clients facing loss and grief. *Psychotherapy in Australia, 9*(2), 30.

Merriam-Webster Dictionary. (n.d.). *Superstition.* (https://www.merriam-webster .com/dictionary/superstition;

Micke, O., Bruns, F., Glatzel, M., Schönekaes, K., Micke, P., Mücke, R., & Büntzel, J. (2009). Predictive factors for the use of complementary and alternative medicine (CAM) in radiation oncology. *European Journal of Integrative Medicine, 1*(1), 19–25.

Mihaela, A. S. (2015). The vision of death in Romanian culture. In J. Cacciatore & J. Defrain (Eds.), *The world of bereavement: Cultural perspectives on death in families* (pp. 121–128). New York, NY: Springer.

Miller-Lewis, L., Tieman, J., Rawlings, D., Parker, D., & Sanderson, C. (2020). Can exposure to online conversations about death and dying influence death competence? an exploratory study within an Australian massive open online course. *OMEGA-Journal of Death and Dying, 81*(2), 242–271.

Molassiotis, A., Scott, J. A., Kearney, N., Pud, D., Magri, M., Selvekerova, S., Bruyns, I., Fernadez-Ortega, P., Panteli, V., Margulies, A., Gudmundsdottir, G., Milovics, L., Ozden, G., Platin, N., & Patiraki, E. (2006). Complementary and alternative medicine use in breast cancer patients in Europe. *Supportive Care in Cancer, 14*(3), 260–267.

Moore, P. J. (2003). The black church: A natural resource for bereavement support. *Journal of Pastoral Counseling, 38,* 47.

Morgan, J. D. (1995). Living our dying and our grieving: Historical and cultural attitudes. In: Wass, H., Neimeyer, R.A. (Eds.), *Dying: facing the facts. 3rd ed.* Washington: Taylor and Francis.

Muecke, R., Paul, M., Conrad, C., Stoll, C., Muenstedt, K., Micke, O., Prott, F.J., Buentzel, J., Huebner, J., & PRIO (Working Group Prevention and Integrative Oncology of the German Cancer Society). (2016). Complementary and alternative medicine in palliative care: A comparison of data from surveys among patients and professionals. *Integrative Cancer Therapies, 15*(1), 10–16.

Mukerjee, S. (1999). *Woman's Death on Husband's Pyre Inspires Hindus.* https://www.latimes.com/archives/la-xpm-1999-dec-26-mn-47664-story.html/

Munet-Vilaro, F. (1998). Grieving and death rituals of Latinos. Paper presented at the *Oncology Nursing Forum, 25*(10), 1761–1763.

National Cancer Institute. (n.d.). *Complementary and alternative medicine.* http://www.cancer.gov/cancertopics/cam/

National Funeral Directors Association. (2019). *Statistics.* https://www.nfda.org/news/statistics/

Neimeyer, R. A. (2001). Reauthoring life narratives: Grief therapy as meaning reconstruction. *The Israel Journal of Psychiatry and Related Sciences, 38*(3/4), 171.

Neimeyer, R. A., & Sands, D. C. (2011). Meaning reconstruction in bereavement: From principles to practice. In R. A. Neimeyer, D. L. Harris, H. R. Winokuer, & G. F. Thornton (Eds.), *Series in death, dying and bereavement. Grief and bereavement in contemporary society: Bridging research and practice* (pp. 9–22). Routledge/Taylor & Francis Group.

Nelson, V. J. (2008). *Professor delivered a moving 'last lecture.'* https://www.latimes.com/archives/la-xpm-2008-jul-26-me-pausch26-story.html

New Zealand Office of Statistics. Population. https://www.stats.govt.nz/topics/population/

Ngata, P. (2005). Death, dying, and grief: A Maori perspective. In J. Morgan & P. Laungani (Eds.), *Death and bereavement around the world* (pp. 29–38). Amityville, New York: Baywood Publishers.

Nobles, W. W. (2006). *Seeking the Sakhu: Foundational writings for an African psychology.* Chicago, IL: Third World Press.

Norenzayan, A., Atran, S., Faulkner, J., & Schaller, M. (2006). Memory and mystery: The cultural selection of minimally counterintuitive narratives. *Cognitive Science, 30*(3), 531–553.

Northcott, H. C., & Wilson, D. M. (2016). *Dying and death in Canada.* Toronto, Canada: University of Toronto Press.

Onukwugha, E., & Alfandre, D. (2019). Against medical advice discharges are increasing for targeted conditions of the Medicare hospital readmissions reduction program. *Journal of General Internal Medicine, 34*(4), 515–517.

Oregon Government Health Authority. (2020, March 6). *Oregon Death with Dignity Act: Annual Report*. https://www.oregon.gov/oha/ph/providerpartnerresources /evaluationresearch/deathwithdignityact/pages/ar-index.aspx/

Organdonor.gov. (n.d.). *The deceased donation process*. https://www.organdonor.gov /about/process/deceased-donation.html/

Padilla, R., Gomez, V., Biggerstaff, S. L., & Mehler, P. S. (2001). Use of curanderismo in a public health care system. *Archives of Internal Medicine, 161*(10), 1336–1340.

Parashar, A. (2008). Gender inequality and religious personal laws in India. *The Brown Journal of World Affairs, 14*(2), 103–112.

Parry, J. K., & Ryan, A. S. (Eds.). (1995). *A cross-cultural look at death, dying, and religion*. Chicago, IL: Nelson-Hall Publishers.

Pathak, N., Raut, A., & Vaidya, A. (2008). Acute cervical pain syndrome resulting from suppressed sneezing. *J Assoc Physicians India, 56,* 728-729.

Pavlov, I. (1977). Classical conditioning. *Learning and Instruction, 4,* 26.

Pewforum. (2015). *Sub-saharan Africa*. https://www.pewforum.org/2015/04/02 /sub-saharan-africa/

Pewforum.org. (2014). *Religion in Latin America*. https://www.pewforum.org/2014 /11/13/religion-in-latin-america/

Pewforum.org. (2011). *Regional distribution of Christians*. https://www.pewforum.org /2011/12/19/global-christianity-regions/

Pew Research Center. (2018). *How do European countries differ in religious commitment?* https://www.pewresearch.org/fact-tank/2018/12/05/how-do-european -countries-differ-in-religious-commitment/

Pew Research Center. (2017). *World's Muslim population more widespread than you might think*. https://www.pewresearch.org/fact-tank/2017/01/31/worlds-muslim -population-more-widespread-than-you-might-think/

Pew Research Center. (2013). *The world's Muslims: religion, politics and society*. https: //assets.pewresearch.org/wp-content/uploads/sites/11/2013/04/worlds-muslims -religion-politics-society-full-report.pdf)

Pew Research Center. (2012). *The global religious landscape*. https://www.pewforum .org/2012/12/18/global-religious-landscape-exec/

Pew Research Center. (2010a). *Muslim population of Indonesia*. https://www.pewforum .org/2010/11/04/muslim-population-of-indonesia/

Pew Research Center. (2010b). *Tolerance and tension: Islam and Christianity in Sub-Saharan Africa*. https://www.pewforum.org/2010/04/15/executive-summary-islam -and-christianity-in-sub-saharan-africa/

Phelan, A., McCarthy, S., & Adams, E. (2018). Examining missed care in community nursing: A cross section survey design. *Journal of Advanced Nursing, 74*(3), 626–636.

Phillips, D. (2015). Afro-Brazilian religions struggle against evangelical hostility. *Washington Post, 6.*

Piaget, J. (1976). Piaget's theory. *Piaget and his school* (pp. 11–23). New York: Springer.

Picheto, R. (2020). CNN. *Coronavirus global death toll passes 300,000 as countries wait in lockdown.* https://www.cnn.com/2020/05/14/world/coronavirus-global-death -toll-300000-intl/index.html/

Plante, T. G. (2010). *Contemplative practices in action: Spirituality, meditation, and health.* Praeger/ABC-CLIO.

Plushnick-Masti, R. (2008, July 25). Prof whose "last lecture" became a sensation dies. *The Sydney Morning Herald. Associated Press.* https://www.smh.com.au /technology/prof-whose-last-lecture-became-a-sensation-dies-20080726-3l6s .html

Post, S., & Neimark, J. (2008). *Why good things happen to good people: How to live a longer, healthier, happier life by the simple act of giving.* New York: Broadway Books.

Procon.org. (2016). *Euthanasia and physician-assisted suicide around the world.* https://euthanasia.procon.org/euthanasia-physician-assisted-suicide-around-the -world/

Puchalski, C. M., & Donnell, E. (2005). Religious and spiritual beliefs in end of life care: How major religions view death and dying. *Techniques in Regional Anesthesia and Pain Management, 9*(3), 114–121.

Qamar, A. H. (2013). The concept of the "evil' and the "evil eye" in Islam and Islamic faith-healing traditions. *Journal of Islamic Thought and Civilization (JITC), 3*(2), 44–53.

Qin, S., & Xia, Y. (2015). Grieving rituals and beliefs of Chinese families. In J. Cacciatore & J. DeFrain (Eds.), *The world of bereavement: cultural perspectives on death in families* (pp. 69–80). New York: Springer.

Ra'Anan, S. B., & Reed, A. Y. (2004). *Heavenly realms and earthly realities in late antique religions.* Cambridge, UK: Cambridge University Press.

Ramadan, T. (2010). *The quest for meaning: Developing a philosophy of pluralism.* Rushden, England: Penguin UK.

Rando, T. A. (1995). Grief and mourning: Accommodating to loss. In H. Wass & R. Neimeyer (Eds.), *Dying: Facing the facts* (pp. 211–242). Washington, DC: Taylor and Francis.

Raudon, S. (2011). *Contemporary funerals and mourning practices: An investigation of five secular countries.* Winston Churchill Memorial Trust.

Rawlings, D., Litster, C., Miller-Lewis, L., Tieman, J., & Swetenham, K. (2020). The voices of death doulas about their role in end of life care. *Health & Social Care in the Community, 28*(1), 12–21.

Ray, B. (1980). The story of Kintu: Myth, death, and ontology in Buganda. *Karp I and Bird CS, Explorations in African Systems of Thought,* 60–79.

Reuters. (2007). *"Dead" man wakes up under autopsy knife.* https://www.reuters.com /article/us-autopsy/dead-man-wakes-up-under-autopsy-knife-idUSN1499758200 70917/

Rey, T., & Stepick, A. (2013). *Crossing the water and keeping the faith: Haitian religion in Miami.* New York: NYU Press.

Richardson, R. (2000). *Death, dissection and the destitute.* Chicago: University of Chicago Press.

Rigpa. (n.d.). https://www.rigpa.org/:

Rocque, G. B., Pisu, M., Jackson, B. E., Kvale, E. A., Demark-Wahnefried, W., Martin, M. Y., Meneses, K., Li, Y., Taylor, R.A., Acemgil, A., Williams, C. P., Lisovicz, N., Fouad, M., Kenzik, K.M., & Partridge, E. E. (2017). Resource use and Medicare costs during lay navigation for geriatric patients with cancer. *JAMA Oncology, 3*(6), 817–825.

Rodriguez, A. (2019). *A Catholic priest condemned a teen's suicide at his own funeral. Now, his mom is suing.* USA Today. https://www.usatoday.com/story/news/nation /2019/11/20/michigan-mom-sues-priest-condemning-sons-suicide-funeral /4246968002/

Rogers, C. H., Floyd, F. J., Seltzer, M. M., Greenberg, J., & Hong, J. (2008). Long-term effects of the death of a child on parents' adjustment in midlife. *Journal of Family Psychology, 22*(2), 203.

Rom, O., & Reznick, A. Z. (2015). The stress reaction: A historical perspective. In M. Pokorski (Ed.), *Respiratory contagion* (pp. 1–4). New York: Springer.

Rosario, A. M., & De La Rosa, M. (2014). Santeria as an informal psychosocial support among Latinas living with cancer. *J Relig Spiritual Soc Work, 33*(1), 4–18.

Rosenblatt, P. C., & Wallace, B. R. (2005). Narratives of grieving African-Americans about racism in the lives of deceased family members. *Death Studies, 29*(3), 217–235.

Ross, C. A. (2010). Hypothesis: The electrophysiological basis of evil eye belief. *Anthropology of Consciousness, 21*(1), 47–57.

Roudi-Fahami, F., & Moghadam, V. M. (2009). *Empowering Women, Developing Society: Female Education in the Middle East and North Africa.* Population Reference Bureau, Washington DC, USA. https://doi.org/10.32380/alrj.v0i0.221

Rowland, C., Hanratty, B., Pilling, M., van den Berg, B., & Grande, G. (2017). The contributions of family care-givers at end of life: A national post-bereavement census survey of cancer carer's hours of care and expenditures. *Palliative Medicine, 31*(4), 346–355.

Ryan, R. M., & Deci, E. L. (2017). *Self-determination theory: Basic psychological needs in motivation, development, and wellness.* New York: Guilford Press.

Sabra, M. (2016). *Marriage first, love later?* https://www.dandc.eu/en/article/fewer-arranged-marriages-arab-countries/

Sass, H. (1992). Criteria for death: Self-determination and public policy. *The Journal of Medicine and Philosophy, 17*(4), 445–454.

Schafer, C. (2011). Celebrant ceremonies: Life-centered funerals in Aotearoa/New Zealand. *Journal of Ritual Studies, 25*(1), 1–13.

Schmidt-Leukel, P. (2006). *Buddhism, Christianity and the question of creation: Karmic or divine?* Hants, England: Ashgate Publishing, Ltd.

Schoulte, J. (2011). Bereavement among African Americans and Latino/a Americans. *Journal of Mental Health Counseling, 33*(1), 11–20.

Schram, R. (2007). Sit, cook, eat, full stop: Religion and the rejection of ritual in Auhelawa (Papua New Guinea). *Oceania, 77*(2), 172–190.

Schwartz, C. E., & Sendor, R. M. (1999). Helping others helps oneself: Response shift effects in peer support. *Social Science & Medicine, 48*(11), 1563–1575.

Schwartz, S. H. (1994). Are there universal aspects in the structure and contents of human values? *Journal of Social Issues, 50*(4), 19–45.

Schwartz, S. H. (2007). Value orientations: Measurement, antecedents and consequences across nations. In R. Jowell, C. Roberts, R. Fitzgerald, & G. Eva (Eds.), *Measuring attitudes cross-nationally: Lessons from the European social survey* (pp. 161–193). London: Sage.

Schwartz, S. H. (2017). The refined theory of basic values. In S. Roccas & L. Sagiv (Eds.), *Values and behavior: Taking a cross cultural perspective* (pp. 51–72). New York: Springer.

Schwartz, S. H., & Bilsky, W. (1990). Toward a theory of the universal content and structure of values: Extensions and cross-cultural replications. *Journal of Personality and Social Psychology, 58*(5), 878.

Schwass, M. (2005). *Last words: Approaches to death in New Zealand's cultures and faiths.* Welllington, New Zealand: Bridget Williams Books.

Sebai, Z. A., Milaat, W. A., & Al-Zulaibani, A. A. (2001). Health care services in Saudi Arabia: Past, present and future. *Journal of Family & Community Medicine, 8*(3), 19.

Sekulska, K. (2019). *Italian funerals: Traditions, songs & what to expect.* https://www.joincake.com/blog/italian-funeral/

Seligman, M. E. P. (1975). *Helplessness: On depression, development, and health.* San Francisco and New York: W. H. Freeman.

Selman, R. L. (1980). *Growth of interpersonal understanding.* New York: Academic Press.

Selye, H. (1973). The evolution of the stress concept: The originator of the concept traces its development from the discovery in 1936 of the alarm reaction to modern therapeutic applications of syntoxic and catatoxic hormones. *American Scientist, 61*(6), 692–699.

Setzer, N. (1985). Brain death: Physiologic definitions. *Critical Care Clinics, 1*(2), 375–396.

Sharma, H., Jagdish, V., Anusha, P., & Bharti, S. (2013). End-of-life care: Indian perspective. *Indian Journal of Psychiatry, 55*(Suppl 2), S293.

Shear, K., Frank, E., Houck, P. R., & Reynolds, C. F. (2005). Treatment of complicated grief: A randomized controlled trial. *JAMA, 293*(21), 2601–2608.

Shear, M. K. (2012). Grief and mourning gone awry: Pathway and course of complicated grief. *Dialogues in Clinical Neuroscience, 14*(2), 119.

Sheikh, A., & Gatrad, A. R. (2008). *Caring for Muslim patients.* Abingdon, England: Radcliffe Medical Press.

Simpson, G. E. (1980). *Black religions in the new world.* New York: Columbia University Press.

Skinner, B. F. (1938). *The behavior of organisms.* New York: Appleton-Century,

Smith, R. J. (1974). *Ancestor worship in contemporary Japan.* Stanford, CA: Stanford University Press.

Smith, T. B., McCullough, M. E., & Poll, J. (2003). Religiousness and depression: Evidence for a main effect and the moderating influence of stressful life events. *Psychological Bulletin, 129*(4), 614.

Spector, R. E. (2002). Cultural diversity in health and illness. *Journal of Transcultural Nursing, 13*(3), 197–199.

Spiby, H., Mcleish, J., Green, J., & Darwin, Z. (2016). 'The greatest feeling you get, knowing you have made a big difference': Survey findings on the motivation and experiences of trained volunteer doulas in England. *BMC Pregnancy and Childbirth, 16*(1), 289.

Statistics Canada. (n.d.). *Census Profile 2016 Census.* https://www12.statcan.gc.ca /census-recensement/2016/dppd/prof/details/page.cfm?Lang=E&Geo1=PR &Code1=01&Geo2=PR&Code2=01&Data=Count&SearchText=canada &SearchType=Begins&SearchPR=01&B1=All&TABID=1

Steele, C. M., Spencer, S. J., & Aronson, J. (2002). Contending with group image: The psychology of stereotype and social identity threat. *Advances in Experimental Social Psychology, 34,* 379–440.

Steen, T. W., & Mazonde, G. N. (1999). Ngaka ya setswana, ngaka ya sekgoa or both? health seeking behaviour in Batswana with pulmonary tuberculosis. *Social Science & Medicine, 48*(2), 163–172.

Stroebe, M., & Schut, H. (1999). The dual process model of coping with bereavement: Rationale and description. *Death Studies, 23*(3), 197–224.

Stroebe, M., & Schut, H. (2005). To continue or relinquish bonds: A review of consequences for the bereaved. *Death Studies, 29*(6), 477–494.

Sudarkasa, N. (1997). African American families and family values. In H. P. McAdoo (Ed.), *Black families* (pp. 9–40). Sage Publications, Inc. (Reprinted in modified form from N. Sudarkasa et al. (Eds.), "Exploring the African-American Experience," Lincoln, PA: Lincoln University Press.

Sullivan, M. A. (1995). May the circle be unbroken: The African American experience of death, dying, and spirituality. *A Cross-Cultural Look at Death, Dying, and Religion.* Chicago, IL: Nelson-Hall Publishers.

Suriname General Bureau of Statistic. (n.d.). *Statistics.* www.statistics-suriname.org

Tagg, T. (2017). *The five people to forgive before you die.* https://www.huffpost.com /entry/the-five-people-to-forgiv_b_9439370/

Tayeb, M. A., Al-Zamel, E., Fareed, M. M., & Abouellail, H. A. (2010). A good death: Perspectives of Muslim patients and health care providers. *Annals of Saudi Medicine, 30*(3), 215–221.

Taylor, R. J., Chatters, L. M., & Jackson, J. S. (2007). Religious and spiritual involvement among older African Americans, Caribbean blacks, and non-Hispanic whites: Findings from the national survey of American life. *The Journals of Gerontology Series B: Psychological Sciences and Social Sciences, 62*(4), S238–S250.

Taylor, R. M. (1997). Reexamining the definition and criteria of death. Paper presented at the *Seminars in Neurology, 17*(03), 265–270.

The Economist Intelligence Unit. (2015). *The 2015 Quality of Death Index Country profiles.* https://eiuperspectives.economist.com/sites/default/files/images/2015 %20Qual ity%20of%20Death%20Index%20Country%20Profiles_Oct%206%20FINAL.pdf

The Grove Hotel. (n.d.). *The Grove.* http://www.thegrovebournemouth.co.uk/

The Hindu. (March 29, 2016). *India's religions by numbers.* https://www.thehindu .com/news/national/religious-communities-census-2011-what-the-numbers-say /article7582284.ece.

Thrane, S. (2010). Hindu end of life: Death, dying, suffering, and karma. *Journal of Hospice & Palliative Nursing, 12*(6), 337–342.

Tmzsports. (2020). *STEPHEN JACKSON to George Floyd's Daughte 'I'LL WALK YOU DOWN THE AISLE ONE DAY.'* https://www.tmz.com/2020/06/02/stephen-jackson -mlb-nfl-owners-nba-justice-george-floyd-video/).

Torp-Kõivupuu, M. (2003). Surmakultuuri muutumine ajas: Ajaloolise võrumaa matusekombestiku näitel [change of death culture across time on the example of burial customs of võrumaa]. tallinna pedagoogikaülikooli toimetised. A 22. *Humaniora.Tallinn,*

Triandis, H. C. (1995). *Individualism and collectivism (New directions in social psychology).* Boulder, CO: Westview Press.

Turner-Weeden, P. (1995). Death and dying from a native American perspective. *The Hospice Journal, 10*(2), 11–13.

UN. (2019). *World economic situation and prospects.* https://www.un.org/development /desa/dpad/wp-content/uploads/sites/45/WESP2019_BOOK-ANNEX-en.pdf/

UNAIDS. (2019). *Global HIV & AIDS statistics—2019 fact sheet.* https://www.unaids .org/en/resources/fact-sheet.

UNICEF. (2019). *Under-five mortality.* https://data.unicef.org/topic/child-survival /under-five-mortality/

University of Vermont Continuing and Distant Education. (n.d.). *End-of-life Doula Professional certificate.* https://learn.uvm.edu/program/end-of-life-doula-at-uvm /end-of-life-doula-certificate/

Unruh, A. M. (2007). Spirituality, religion, and pain. *Canadian Journal of Nursing Research Archive, 39*(2).

US Census Bureau: *Quickfacts.* https://www.census.gov/quickfacts/fact/table/US /RHI125218/

Utter, J. (2002). *American Indians: Answers to today's questions* (2nd ed.). Norman, OK: University of Oklahoma Press.

Valk, U. (2006). Ghostly possession and real estate: The dead in contemporary Estonian folklore. *Journal of Folklore Research, 43*(1), 31–51.

Van der Geest, S. (2000). Funerals for the living: Conversations with elderly people in Kwahu, Ghana. *African Studies Review, 43*(3), 103–129.

Van der Pijl, Y. (2016). Death in the family revisited: Ritual expression and controversy in a creole transnational mortuary sphere. *Ethnography, 17*(2), 147–167.

Van der Pijl, Y. (2010). Pentecostal-charismatic Christianity: African-Surinamese perceptions and experiences. *Exchange, 39*(2), 179–195.

Velho, G. (2003). *Anthropology of complex societies. Project Metamorfose* (3rd ed.) (Jorge Zahar, Ed.). Rio De Janeiro, Brasil.

Watson, P. (2002). *Waiting to die on banks of a river of salvation.* https://www.latimes .com/archives/la-xpm-2002-nov-24-fg-widows24-story.html

Watt, W. M. (2014). *Introduction to the qur'an.* Edinburgh, UK: Edinburgh University Press.

Weiss, R. S. (1988). Loss and recovery. *Journal of Social Issues, 44*(3), 37–52.

WHO. (2020). *Road traffic injuries.* https://www.who.int/news-room/fact-sheets/detail /road-traffic-injuries/

WHO. (2018). *The top 10 causes of death.* https://www.who.int/news-room/fact-sheets/detail/the-top-10-causes-of-death/

WHO. (2004). *The world health report 2004–changing history.* Geneva: The Organization.

Wiech, K., Farias, M., Kahane, G., Shackel, N., Tiede, W., & Tracey, I. (2008). An fMRI study measuring analgesia enhanced by religion as a belief system. *Pain, 139*(2), 467–476.

Willson, G., McIntosh, A. J., Morgan, A., & Sanders, D. (2018). Terminal illness and tourism: A review of current literature and directions for future research. *Tourism Recreation Research, 43*(2), 268–272.

Winston, C. A. (2003). African American grandmothers parenting grandchildren orphaned by AIDS: Grieving and coping with loss. *Illness, Crisis & Loss, 11*(4), 350–361.

Worden, J. W. (2008). *Grief counseling and grief therapy: A handbook for the mental health practitioner.* New York: Springer.

World Bank. (2020). *World Bank country and lending groups.* https://datahelpdesk.worldbank.org/knowledgebase/articles/906519-world-bank-country-and-lending-groups/

World Bank. (2018a). *Population, total.* https://data.worldbank.org/indicator/sp.pop.totl/

World Bank. (2018b). *Population, total–Suriname.* https://data.worldbank.org/indicator/SP.POP.TOTL?locations=SR/

Worth, A., Irshad, T., Bhopal, R., Brown, D., Lawton, J., Grant, E., Murray, S., Kendall, M., Adam, J., Gardee, R., & Sheikh, A. (2009). Vulnerability and access to care for South Asian Sikh and Muslim patients with life limiting illness in Scotland: Prospective longitudinal qualitative study. *Bmj, 338,* b183.

Wu, N. (2020). *Trump says George Floyd 'hopefully' looking down and saying 'this is a great thing that's happening'. USA Today.* https://www.usatoday.com/story/news/politics/2020/06/05/trump-economy-event-george-floyd-hopefully-looking-down/3154495001/

Wujastyk, D. (2003). *The roots of Ayurveda: Selections from Sanskrit medical writings.* New York: Penguin.

Yan, H., & Bowman, R. (2019). CNN. *A priest condemned suicide while speaking at a teen's funeral. Now a grieving mother is suing him.* https://www.cnn.com/2019/11/20/us/michigan-mom-sues-priest-for-condemning-suicide-at-funeral/index.html

Yates, F. E., & Benton, L. A. (1995). Biological senescence: Loss of integration and resilience. *Canadian Journal on Aging/La Revue Canadienne Du Vieillissement, 14*(1), 106–120.

Younoszai, B. (1993). Mexican American perspectives related to death. In D. P. Irish, K. F. Lundquist, & V. J. Nelson (Eds.), *Ethnic variations in dying, death, and grief: Diversity in universality* (pp. 67–78). New York: Taylor & Francis.

Zeller, T., Muenstedt, K., Stoll, C., Schweder, J., Senf, B., Ruckhaeberle, E., Becker, S., Serve, H., & Huebner, J. (2013). Potential interactions of complementary and alternative medicine with cancer therapy in outpatients with gynecological cancer in a comprehensive cancer center. *Journal of Cancer Research and Clinical Oncology, 139*(3), 357–365.

Zeng, Y. S., Wang, C., Ward, K. E., & Hume, A. L. (2018). Complementary and alternative medicine in hospice and palliative care: A systematic review. *Journal of Pain and Symptom Management, 56*(5), 781–794. e4.

Zheng, N. T., Mukamel, D. B., Caprio, T., Cai, S., & Temkin-Greener, H. (2011). Racial disparities in in-hospital death and hospice use among nursing home residents at the end-of-life. *Medical Care, 49*(11), 992.

NAME INDEX

SUBJECT INDEX

CHARLES C THOMAS · PUBLISHER · LTD.

TEACHING ENGLISH LEARNERS IN INCLUSIVE CLASSROOMS
(4th Edition)
by Elva Duran
438 pp. (7 x 10) • 19 illustrations • 27 tables
$49.95 (paper) • $49.95 (ebook)

PARENTAL ALIENATION — SCIENCE AND LAW
by Demosthenes Lorandos and William Bernet
682 pp. (7 x 10) • 4 illustrations • 12 tables
$74.95 (hard) • $74.95 (ebook)

WHEN PARENTS HAVE PROBLEMS (3rd Edition)
by Susan B. Miller
130 pp. (7 x 10)
$19.95 (paper) • $19.95 (ebook)

POSITIVE BEHAVIOR SUPPORTS FOR ADULTS WITH DISABILITIES IN EMPLOYMENT, COMMUNITY, AND RESIDENTIAL SETTINGS (2nd Edition)
by Keith Storey and Michal Post
240 pp. (7 x 10) • 9 illustrations • 29 tables
$38.95 (paper) • $38.95 (ebook)

UNDERSTANDING PARENTAL ALIENATION
by Karen Woodall and Nick Woodall
252 pp. (7 x 10) • 6 illustrations
$39.95 (paper) • $39.95 (ebook)

THE SOCIOLOGY OF DEVIANCE (2nd Edition)
by Robert J. Franzese
398 pp. (7 x 10) • 21 illustrations • 6 tables
$64.95 (paper) • $64.95 (ebook)

TWENTY-FIRST CENTURY DYNAMICS OF MULTICULTURALISM
by Martin Guevara Urbina
372 pp. (7 x 10) • 16 illustrations • 1 table
$59.95 (paper) • $59.95 (ebook)

CULTURAL DIVERSITY, INCLUSION AND JUSTICE
by George Henderson
238 pp. (7 x 10)
$37.95 (paper) • $37.95 (ebook)

THE HANDBOOK OF CHILD LIFE
(2nd Edition)
by Richard H. Thompson
642 pp. (7 x 10) • 7 illustrations • 14 tables
$59.95 (paper) • $59.95 (ebook)

SOCIAL WORK IN JUVENILE AND CRIMINAL JUSTICE SYSTEMS
(4th Edition)
by David W. Springer and Albert R. Roberts
418 pp. (8 x 10) • 30 illustrations • 17 tables
$64.95 (paper) • $64.95 (ebook)

CHOOSING TO LIVE
by Cliff Williams
204 pp. (7 x 10) • 1 illustration
$28.95 (paper) • $28.95 (ebook)

INTRODUCTION TO HUMAN RELATIONS STUDIES
by George Henderson and Wesley C. Long
364 pp. (7 x 10)
$62.95 (paper) • $62.95 (ebook)

EMIGRATING FROM CHINA TO THE UNITED STATES (2nd Edition)
by Yushi (Boni) Li
270 pp. (7 x 10) • 36 illustrations
$34.95 (paper) • $34.95 (ebook)

SOCIAL WORK IN JUVENILE AND CRIMINAL JUSTICE SYSTEMS
(4th Edition)
by David W. Springer and Albert R. Roberts
418 pp. (8 x 10) • 30 illustrations • 17 tables
$64.95 (paper) • $64.95 (ebook)

Find us on:

FACEBOOK.COM/CCTPUBLISHER

Sign-up for our eNewsletter for special discounts and new releases at www.ccthomas.com.

FREE SHIPPING ON DOMESTIC RETAIL ORDERS THROUGH OUR WEBSITE!*
*Available on retail purchases through our **website only** to shipping addresses in the Continental United States.

TO ORDER: www.ccthomas.com • books@ccthomas.com • 1-800-258-8980